Radical Theology and the Death of God

Radical Theology
and
The
Death
of
God

Thomas J. J. Altizer
and
William Hamilton

The Bobbs-Merrill Company, Inc.
A Subsidiary of Howard W. Sams & Co., Inc.
Publishers   Indianapolis   New York   Kansas City

Copyright © 1966 by Thomas J. J. Altizer and William Hamilton
All rights reserved
Library of Congress catalog card number 66-20111

Designed by Quentin Fiore
Printed in the United States of America

"American Theology, Radicalism and the Death of God," by William Hamilton, originally published, *Christianity and Crisis*, Dec. 13, 1965; "The Death of God Theologies," by William Hamilton, originally published, *The Christian Scholar*, Spring, 1965; "Banished from the Land of Unity," by William Hamilton, *Journal of Religion*, Oct., 1959; "Thursday's Child," by William Hamilton, originally published, *Theology Today*, Jan., 1964; "America and the Future of Theology," by Thomas J. J. Altizer, originally published, *Antaios*, Sept., 1963; "Theology and the Death of God," by Thomas J. J. Altizer, originally published, *The Centennial Review*, Spring, 1964; "Dietrich Bonhoeffer," by William Hamilton, originally published, *Nation*, April 19, 1965; "Word and History," by Thomas J. J. Altizer, originally published, *Theology Today*, Oct., 1965; "The New Optimism," by William Hamilton, originally published, *Theology Today*, Jan., 1966; "William Blake and the Role of Myth in the Radical Christian Vision," by Thomas J. J. Altizer, originally published, *The Centennial Review*, Fall, 1965.

In Memory of Paul Tillich

Contents

Preface

Radical theology is a contemporary development within Protestantism—with some Jewish, Roman Catholic and non-religious response and participation already forming—which is carrying the careful openness of the older theologies toward atheism a step further. It is, in effect, an attempt to set an atheist point of view within the spectrum of Christian possibilities. While radical theology in this sense has not yet become a self-conscious "movement," it nevertheless has gained the interest and in part the commitment of a large number of Christians in America, particularly from students of all disciplines, and from the younger ranks of teachers and pastors. The aim of the new theology is not simply to seek relevance or contemporaneity for its own sake but to strive for a whole new way of theological understanding. Thus it is a theological venture in the strict sense, but it is no less a pastoral response hoping to give support to those who have chosen to live as Christian atheists.

The phrase "death of God" has quite properly become a watchword, a stumbling-block, and something of a test in radical theology, which itself is a theological expression of a contemporary Christian affirmation of the death of God. Radical theology thus best interprets itself when it begins to say what it means by that phrase. The task of clarifying the possible meanings of the phrase, "death of God," is scarcely begun in the essays of this volume, but no student of Nietzsche will be surprised at this inconclusiveness, recalling the widely different interpretations Nietzsche's proclamation of the death of God has received in the twentieth century. Nor should the phrase "death of God" be linked to Nietzsche alone, for in one way or another it lies at the foundation of a distinctly modern thought and experience.

Perhaps the category of "event" will prove to be the most useful answer to the recurring question, "Just what does 'death of God' refer to?" But not even this specification sufficiently narrows the meaning to make definition possible, and if one wanted to, one could list a range of possible meanings of the phrase along such lines as these, moving slowly from conventional atheism to theological orthodoxy. It might mean:

1. That there is no God and that there never has been. This position is traditional atheism of the old-fashioned kind, and it does seem hard to see how it could be combined, except very unstably, with Christianity or any of the Western religions.

2. That there once was a God to whom adoration, praise and trust were appropriate, possible, and even necessary, but that now there is no such God. This is the position of the death of God or radical theology. It is an atheist position, but with a difference. If there was a God, and if there now isn't, it should be possible to indicate why this change took place, when it took place, and who was responsible for it.

3. That the idea of God and the word God itself are in need of radical reformulation. Perhaps totally new words are needed; perhaps a decent silence about God should be observed; but ultimately, a new treatment of the idea and the word can be expected, however unexpected and surprising it may turn out to be.

4. That our traditional liturgical and theological language needs a thorough overhaul; the reality abides, but classical modes of thought and forms of language may well have had it.

5. That the Christian story is no longer a saving or a healing story. It may manage to stay on as merely illuminating or instructing or guiding, but it no longer performs its classical functions of salvation or redemption. In this

new form, it might help us cope with the demons, but it cannot abolish them.

6. That certain concepts of God, often in the past confused with the classical Christian doctrine of God, must be destroyed: for example, God as problem solver, absolute power, necessary being, the object of ultimate concern.

7. That men do not today experience God except as hidden, absent, silent. We live, so to speak, in the time of the death of God, though that time will doubtless pass.

8. That the gods men make, in their thought and action (false gods or idols, in other words), must always die so that the true object of thought and action, the true God, might emerge, come to life, be born anew.

9. That of a mystical meaning: God must die in the world so that he can be born in us. In many forms of mysticism the death of Jesus on the cross is the time of that worldly death. This is a medieval idea that influenced Martin Luther, and it is probably this complex of ideas that lies behind the German chorale "God Himself is Dead" that may well be the historical source for our modern use of "death of God."

10. Finally, that our language about God is always inadequate and imperfect.

There are other pressing questions in addition to the one about the meaning of the phrase. If the death of God is an event of some kind, *when* did it happen and *why?* In response to this sort of self-query, radical theology is being more and more drawn into the disciplines of intellectual history and literary criticism to answer the "when" question, and into philosophy and the behavioral sciences to answer the "why" question. One of the major research tasks now facing the radical theologians is a thorough-going systematic interpretation of the meaning of the death of God in nineteenth-century European and American thought and literature, from, say, the French Revolution to Freud. This means finding a common principle of interpretation to handle such divergent strands as the new history and its consequent historicism, romantic poetry from Blake to Goethe, Darwin and evolutionism, Hegel and the Hegelian left, Marx and Marxism, psychoanalysis, the many varieties of more recent literature including such divergent figures as Dostoevsky, Strindberg and Baudelaire, and, of course, Nietzsche himself.

Of course the questions "why did it happen" and "when did it happen" cannot fully be answered in nineteenth-century terms. Nevertheless, it is increasingly true that the nineteenth century is to radical theology what the sixteenth century was to Protestant neo-orthodoxy. For only in the nineteenth century do we find the death of God lying at the very center of vision and experience. True, we can learn a great deal about the death of God in the history of religions, if only because gods have always been in the process of dying, from the time the sky gods fell into animism to the disappearance of a personal or individual deity in the highest expression of mysticism. Yet, it is in Christianity and Christianity alone that we find a radical or consistent doctrine of the Incarnation. Only the Christian can celebrate an Incarnation in which God has actually become flesh, and radical theology must finally understand the Incarnation itself as effecting the death of God. Although the death of God may not have been historically actualized or realized until the nineteenth century, the radical theologian cannot dissociate this event from Jesus and his original proclamation.

The radical theologian has a strange but compelling interest in the figure of Jesus. This must not be confused with the nineteenth-century liberal quest for the historical Jesus. The new theologian has died to the liberal tradition and is in quest of that Jesus who appears in conjunction with the death of God. Radical theology is peculiarly a product of the mid-twentieth century; it has been initiated by Barth and neo-orthodoxy into a form of theology which can exist in the midst of the collapse of Christendom and the advent of secular atheism. It has also learned from Paul Tillich and Rudolf Bultmann the necessity for theology to engage in a living dialogue with the actual world and history which theology confronts. Finally, we cannot fail to add that radical theology, as here conceived, has a distinctively American form. It reflects the situation of a Christian life in a seemingly neutral but almost totally secular culture and society. Hopefully it also reflects the choice of those Christians who have chosen to live in Christ in a world come of age.

The following pieces have little in common stylistically, they are addressed to diverse problems, and in large measure embody distinct assumptions and methods. Yet all of these pieces, however various their form, are directed to the one fundamental problem of a Christian theological response to the death of God. The authors offer this book as a contribution to the new theological dialogue which must begin.

January 1, 1966   WILLIAM HAMILTON
                                                     THOMAS J. J. ALTIZER

I
Introductions to
The Radical Theology

*These three pieces provide the most adequate introduction
to the radical theology, insofar as the authors are representative
of it. Each of them was written in response to a request. The
first, "American Theology, Radicalism and the Death of God,"
is a journalistic and deliberately controversial response to a
request from* Christianity and Crisis *to prepare a "new trends
in theology" article. It appeared in late 1965, and serves to
set the radical theology in relation to other lively Protestant
options.*   W.H.

American Theology, Radicalism and the Death of God

Christianity and Crisis recently began a series about new forms of American theology. This is a good thing—good for *Christianity and Crisis* because some of its friends had begun to suspect that it was becoming the house organ for spirited defenses of the theological and ethical consensus in Protestantism. And good for American theology because new lines between theology and the rest of the academic, ecclesiastical and cultural community are badly needed right now. It is important not to be satisfied with the news magazines, the weekly religious journals and *The New Yorker*.

Funny things are happening to theology in America. *First,* it is a far less important discipline today than it has been for some time. This means that the seminary, the place where theological work is usually done, has also become less important. The theological movement called neo-orthodoxy was centered there. During the time of its hegemony the seminary was the most exciting place to be, and it tended to look down on the church, the college religion department, the student movement, councils of churches. But today, seminary students— the best ones at least—are more interested in the Street than in the Academy or the Temple. For many of them theology has become a charming but minor art and the seminary a way station.

The disappearance of both theology and seminary from their central position can be demonstrated by noticing where the really exciting Protestant work is being done on the racial issue today: seminaries have shown themselves quite incapable

3

of creative institutional action, while groups from national and local councils of churches are providing the brains, the guts and the leadership.

Second, theology in America is not only losing its prestige, it is changing its mode of communication. Until quite recently it was a solid, slow moving "book-discipline," an academic discipline in which most of the important material was published in hardcover books.

This no longer seems to be the case. Developments are too fast moving for books or for solid quarterly articles which often take as long between writing and publication as do books. Also, many quarterlies, monthlies and weeklies contain so much filler and hasty work that it is not easy to find the solid stuff.

In this period of rapid theological change no satisfactory means of information-passing has been devised. Communication is by telephone calls, improvised luncheon meetings attended by people who have cut an important conference session, and letter-writing (my guess would be that the key to America's future lies somewhere in private letters). Unlike the biblical people, who seem to have mastered this art of finding out what articles are going to say before they are published, theologians are still perplexed by these changes.

Third, no agreement has been reached on what is behind the sense of swift change or on what things are changing *to.* However, this seems to me roughly what the situation is:

There are four camps; the lines dividing them are porous, and some have pitched their tents on the boundaries. A large group *still* feels at home in the ecumenical, Barthian, neo-Reformation tradition. Most of the American contributions to the ecumenical movement lie here, as do most of the Protestants engaged in dialogue with the Roman Catholics.

This position may become more important in disciplines ancillary to theology than in theology itself; as liberalism left systematic theology and went to live with psychology of religion and Christian education for a while, so neo-orthodoxy may have its immediate future in history of doctrine, Old Testament and perhaps in ethics.

For instance, one of the most interesting recent events was the reception in some circles of Harvey Cox's elegant pastiche *The Secular City* (pop Barth?) as a new language for this neo-orthodox tradition. This admirable book came, one might say, as a cool glass of salt water to the thirsty Establishment.

The second group contains the Bultmannians and new hermeneutics people; a great deal of solid New Testament work is, of course, being done under this banner. Theologically it is exciting and unstable, particularly at the left margin, where a drift to the third or fourth groups is discernible.

Third is the group which is hopeful for a new kind of natural, metaphysical or philosophical theology. The ontological argument is being restudied; so are Wittgenstein, Whitehead and Heidegger. Looking at this growing, enthusiastic and intelligent group, it is clear that liberal theology is by no means as dead as some of the older funeral orations implied.

The fourth is the radical or "death of God" theological group. A number of names are given to this fourth group, none of which is entirely satisfactory. One hears of the "new" theology, the secular, the radical, the death of God theology. I think radical is perfectly adequate, though there is often a kind of arrogance in ascribing this to oneself. However, if it is used, it should be carefully distinguished from other forms of radicalism. We have *radical* radicals today; they are non-moderate and in general can be identified by their attitudes toward James Baldwin, LeRoi Jones, Martin Luthur King and civil disobedience. There are *sexual* radicals, and they, too, are easy to spot. They are radically uninterested in pre-marital sexual chastity; they believe in being radically open to others, and they are firmly against "Puritanism."

We also have the *ecclesiastical* radicals who say critical things about the present form of the institutional church. Members of this group write study books for the student movement and speak about secular, worldly and non-religious theology. (They are often confused with the theological radicals for this reason.)

The classic statement of this position is found in J. C. Hoekendijk's World Student Christian Federation address at

Strasbourg in 1960. I suspect that a good deal of the interesting neo-orthodox theology in the next few years will be done in this mode. On the whole it is a creative and practical movement. New strategy and new structures may well be forthcoming, but we probably should not expect new theology in the strict sense.

One person may participate in all four of these forms of radicalism, and there is no reason why the term "radical" should not be used for all four, so long as they are distinguished. The name I prefer for theological radicalism is the death of God theology.

The death of God radical theologians, recently given far more visibility than they either desired or deserved, are men without God who do not anticipate his return. But it is not a simple not-having, for there is an experience of loss. Painful for some, not so for others, it is loss nonetheless. The loss is not of the idols, or of the God of theism, but of the God of the Christian tradition. And this group persists, in the face of both bewilderment and fury, in calling itself Christian. It persists in making use of the phrase "death of God," in spite of its rhetorical color, partly because it is a phrase that cannot be adapted to traditional use by the theologians today.

The death of God tradition is beginning to see the work laid out before it: historical, exegetical, apologetic, ethical. It is not out to appeal to modern man or to "take him seriously," nor is it enchanted with being new or relevant. Wisely, it knows that many secular modern men like their theological foes to be as orthodox as possible so they can be rejected as irrelevant. (Known as the Walter Kaufman syndrome, it has recently been repeated by secular critics of Bishop J. A. T. Robinson.)

Some connection may be discernable between the death of God theology and the Jew today, and I would hope it would be possible to set down some theological rules for a Christian, or at least a Protestant, dialogue with the Jew—both secular and believing. Many have noted the psychological affinities between certain kinds of Protestants and certain kinds of Jews (Freud named a son for Oliver Cromwell), and I think this may partly be explained by saying that both the Protestant and the Jew are men caught between a having and a not-having and are never satisfied by a verbal resolution of this plight.

The believing Jew is the man with God and without the Messiah; the death of God Protestant is the man without God but not without something like the Messiah. They may not have much identity of content, but a formal kinship exists that could lead to some levels of theological dialogue not made possible by other forms of Protestant theology.

What is the relation of radical theology to the Church? It certainly must be clear that this theology has neither the power nor the ability to serve the Protestant Church in most of its present institutional forms. I do not see how preaching, worship, prayer, ordination, the sacraments can be taken seriously by the radical theologian. If there is a need for new institutional forms and styles, however, this theology doubtless has a great deal to say. If theology is tested by its ability to shape new kinds of personal and corporate existence in the times in which it lives, then it would seem that radical theology may be able to pass such a test.

The radical theology is beginning to receive criticism, but as yet most of it seems to be composed largely of patronization, accusations of moral flaws (usually arrogance) and warnings against faddishness. The radical theologians are aware of their moral flaws, which seem about the same as those of their friends in other schools of theological thought. And they quite simply deny that this movement can be disposed of as a flashy new fad. Radical theology isn't everything and doesn't claim to be. For the Christian in today's world it claims only to be able to work out a way of "making it."

W. H.

In the spring of 1963 I had just finished my second book,
Mircea Eliade and the Dialectic of the Sacred, *a book
attempting to evolve a theological method for a positive
Christian confrontation with modern atheism. Eliade had asked
me to write an article for* Antaios, *a German cultural and
intellectual journal edited by him and Ernst Jünger. I decided
to seize this opportunity to address myself to the problem of
the distinctive theological vocation of America, taking the
non-theological but sophisticated German reader as a sounding
board for what was for me a new kind of theological writing,
and the result became, "America and the Future of Theology."*

T. J. J. A.

America and the Future of Theology

Observing that the waters of European theology are at present somewhat stagnant, Karl Barth recently said that what we need in Europe and America is not a renewal of an older form of theology but a "theology of freedom" that looks ahead and strives forward. If this indeed is the true task of theology today, then perhaps, at long last, the time has come for America to assume a theological vocation, a vocation previously denied her because America lacks those deep roots in the past which have thus far been an essential presupposition for theological creativity. America is truly a semi-barbarous nation if only because it has no history. Every American can in some sense join James Baldwin in saying that the Chartres cathedral is not part of his past. As Americans, our past is simply an extension of a horizontal present, and apart from a few rapidly vanishing insular regions of the nation, the contemporary American cannot associate a living moment with a moment of the past. Thus the American who is in quest of a deeper form of existence must look forward to the future, not a future which is simply an extension of the present, but a future that will shatter all that we know as present. Hence an anarchistic utopianism has always been a deeply ingrained component of the American character. And it is precisely such a detachment from the past that may now make possible a new form of theology.

On all sides theologians are agreed that we are now in some sense living in a post-Christian age. Catholic theologians can speak of the new challenge posed by the necessity of a post-Constantinian form of the church, while Protestant theologians can vie with one another in detaching faith from all forms of existence in an admittedly secular historical present. Yet few if any theologians confess that our time demands a radical transformation of faith. Rudolf Bultmann's demythologizing stops short of demythologizing the *Kerygma,* and Paul Tillich's method of correlation demands a preservation of the form of the traditional Christian symbols. By preserving faith inviolate from the brute realities of a post-Christian history, theology has isolated faith from history, whether in the orthodox manner of Barth, or via the liberal and semi-existential methods of the dialectical theologians. These methods are semi-existential because no dialectical theologian has been open to a contemporary form of *Existenz,* for dialectical theology has retained the Kierkegaardian thesis that authentic human existence culminates in faith. Kierkegaard conceived of faith as the product of a dialectical negation of time and history, of the "universal," and of "objectivity"; however, his twentieth-century successors have imagined that faith is isolated from history, that faith is independent of an historical ground, and thus is totally autonomous. In the final phase of his work, Kierkegaard pronounced the death knell upon Christendom. While Kierkegaard's attack upon Christendom was the consistent development of his life and thought, he nevertheless knew a moment of inwardness, reached by the negation of objectivity, which was indubitably Christian. Yet Nietzsche's proclamation of the death of God gave witness to the advent of a new historical moment. This moment transformed transcendence into immanence, thereby dissolving the religious ground of subjectivity and inwardness. Authentic contemporary *Existenz* is alienated from faith, or alienated from all historic forms of faith, thus necessitating a non-dialectical retreat of theology from both the inner and the outer realms, from subjectivity and objectivity, from the "inner now" of *Geschichte* and the "outer now" of *Historie.*

While Martin Buber has courageously called for a transformation of faith in response to the "eclipse" of God, Christian theology has chosen to remain silent about the theological import of the death of God. We must not accept the contemporaneity of a form of theology which maintains that the death of God does not affect the inner man, for here lies the Gnostic temptation of a retreat from history. It is precisely the acceptance of Nietzsche's proclamation of the death of God that is the real test of a contemporary form of faith. Tillich, in his early writing, formulated the theological criterion of contemporaneity with his thesis that a Christ who is not contemporary is not the true Christ; that a revelation which demands a leap out of history is not true revelation. But the theological method of the mature Tillich, particularly as contained in the second volume of his *Systematic Theology*, is grounded in the traditional Christian principle that Christ is the "answer" to the *Angst* of the human condition. Once granted that *Existenz* in our time is swallowed up in a radically immanent mode of being, then the Christ who is an "answer" to our condition must be a wholly immanent Word that is fully detached from the Jesus of history. At this point, the positions of both Tillich and Bultmann become ambivalent. Christ is both immanent and transcendent, the Word is simultaneously an immanent Word which is the ground of our *Existenz* and a transcendent Word in full continuity with the historic forms of the Christian faith. From one point of view, we might say that dialectical theology culminates in a simple contradiction. From another, we might rather say that dialectical theology refuses to be truly dialectical, it refuses both radical transcendence (biblical or eschatological faith) and radical immanence (contemporary *Existenz*), and thus is forced to reach a non-dialectical synthesis between a partial transcendence (Tillich's Unconditioned and Bultmann's Word of faith) and a partial immanence (an *Existenz* whose *Angst* can only be answered by "faith").

A theology that chooses to meet our time, a theology that accepts the destiny of history, must first assess the theological significance of the death of God. We must realize that the death of God is an historical event, that God has died in our cosmos, in our history, in our *Existenz*. While there is no immediate necessity in assuming that the God who has died is the God of "faith," there is also no escaping the inevitable consequence that the dead God is not the God of idolatry, or false piety, or "religion," but rather the God of the historic Christian Church, and beyond the Church, of Christendom at large. Why, it may be asked, is it necessary to link in this manner the Church with Christendom? Because when the Church entered the Hellenistic world, and later helped create the world of the modern West, it became indissolubly linked with a particular historical tradition. Again and again modern theologians have found to their great embarrassment that logically and linguistically it is not possible to dissociate the rites, creeds and dogmas of the Church from their Western form. For example, the Christian idea of God is obviously a product of the fusion of the Bible with Greek ontology, and in large measure the distinctiveness of the "Christian God" derives from its Greek roots. The God or Logos who exists in an integral and essential relationship with the world is a non-biblical God, as Barth so forcefully insists, yet this is the God who is most distant from the non-Christian religions, with the exception of those religions, such as Judaism and Islam, which have themselves come under the influence of Greek philosophy. When biblical faith is apprehended in its original form, it loses its radical uniqueness, and no longer exists at such a distance from the higher forms of Oriental religion. Furthermore, modern biblical scholarship has fully demonstrated the chasm which exists between the faith of the historic Church and its biblical ground, a chasm created by the entrance of the Church into history. What we know as the Christian Church is the product of the Bible and history. A fully biblical form of the Church, as the sects have demonstrated, would lose all genuine continuity with the Church of history.

Once again theology must return to Kierkegaard, the real creator of modern theology. Kierkegaard's leap of faith is, of course, a leap out of history; and the necessity of the leap derives from the very existence of Christendom. When Kierkegaard defines faith as "contemporaneity with Christ," he assumes the necessity of this leap, a "leap" which, dialectically, requires a negation of Christendom. But we must not make the non-dialectical assumption that Christendom is simply secularized Christianity. Dialectically, Christendom is everything that Christianity has become in history. Wherever the Christian faith has entered history, there lies Christendom. Thus the Christian God belongs to Christendom. One of the greatest problems in theology lies in the definition of Christendom, that is to say in the realization of the full meaning of the transformation effected in faith by its entrance into history. Shall we come to understand that everything we "know" as Christian is finally Christendom? Or, negatively stated, what can be the residuum of a faith which accepts the death of God? Will faith contain any definable or cognitive meanings? Indeed, will it contain any symbolic meaning? When no "up" or "down" is left, when "beginning" and "end" and all historic symbols have disappeared, what will be the meaning of such primary dogmas as the Incarnation and the Creation? In the Orient, a fully dialectical form of faith, such as Madhyamika Buddhism, has inevitably dissolved all positive meaning, with the result that it has left behind the world of symbols, myths and dogmas. Is this the destiny that awaits the Christian faith? Yet, dialectically, a faith that accepts the death of God must go beyond all previous dialectical forms of faith. Never before has faith been called upon to negate all *religious* meaning, but it is the very radical nature of this negative movement which can prepare the way for the deepest epiphany of faith.

At first glance America would seem to provide little hope that it can meet the awesome challenge now confronting theology. America has no tradition of a rich humanistic scholarship; it has not been an arena of purely theoretical thinking in any field. Most damning of all, America has become the very embodiment of that alienation, *anomie,* and dehumanization which is the curse of existence in a highly technological and urban society (Heidegger has remarked that, metaphysically speaking, America and Russia are the same, for here "time as history" has vanished from human life). Nevertheless, America has provided a haven for innumerable European artists and thinkers. One only has to remember that it was here that Alfred North Whitehead evolved his metaphysical system, and Paul Tillich wrote his *Systematic Theology*. Or that scholars as diverse as Pierre Teilhard de Chardin, Mircea Eliade, and Herbert Marcuse here found a new soil for their work. The one quality which these expatriate Europeans have in common is the radical thrust of their thought. One might imagine that existence in a vacuous society effects a liberation from the past, a liberation that is potentially demonic to be sure, but a liberation that likewise provides the occasion for the deepest kind of creativity. Need we wonder that it was America which was the first country to respond to psychoanalysis, that it was the American poets Ezra Pound and T. S. Eliot who helped initiate a decisive revolution in European poetry, or that it has been America which has been most open to modern scientific thinking? Granted that a mass culture has never reached so low a point as in America, that a vulgar positivism pervades American thought, and that here solitude has become such a luxury that it is to be purchased only with the most arduous resolution. But the American, too, can join the Marxist in speaking of the birth-pangs of revolution. Only here there is little hope of a revolution in society: the one revolution that can justify America is a revolution in thought.

The alienation of the thinker from society is an ancient and a universal theme; perhaps its modern variant is the alienation of thought from society. Ours is a time when the individual person has disappeared, or, at least that form of the person has passed away which was the peculiar creation of Western culture and society. If thought is truly alienated from society then the initial movement of thought must be a negation of society, a negation which establishes thought's right to existence. Today the task of thought is the negation of history, and most particularly the negation of the history created by Western man. But this negation must be dialectical, which means that finally it must be affirmation. A negation that arises out of *ressentiment* is forbidden, forbidden because it is merely destructive.

Dialectical negation must never lose a positive ground. Nor can true negation seek a partial or non-dialectical synthesis; it must spurn a twilight which is merely ideological (ideology, as Marx taught us, is thought which is the reflection of society). In our time, thought must hold its goal in abeyance; otherwise it can scarcely establish itself, and is thereby doomed to be a mere appendix to society. If we accept these strictures for theology, then it follows that contemporary theology must be alienated from the Church, that it can be neither kerygmatic, dogmatic nor apologetic, and thus its deepest immediate task is the discovery of its own ground. Like all thought, theology, too, must find its ground in that terrible "night" unveiled by the death of God. It must return to that mystical "dark night" in which the very presence of God has been removed, but now that "night" is all, no longer can theology find a haven in prayer or meditation. Dietrich Bonhoeffer has said that we must not reach the New Testament too quickly, but the time has now come to say that theology can know neither grace nor salvation; for a time it must dwell in darkness, existing on this side of the resurrection. Consequently the theologian must exist outside of the Church: he can neither proclaim the Word, celebrate the sacraments, nor rejoice in the presence of the Holy Spirit. Before contemporary theology can become itself, it must first exist in silence.

In the presence of a vocation of silence, theology must cultivate the silence of death. To be sure, the death to which theology is called is the death of God. Nor will it suffice for theology to merely accept the death of God. If theology is truly to die, it must *will* the death of God, must *will* the death of Christendom, must freely choose the destiny before it, and therefore must cease to be itself. Everything that theology has thus far become must now be negated; and negated not simply because it is dead, but rather because theology cannot be reborn unless it passes through, and freely wills, its own death and dissolution.

Paradoxically, theology is now impelled to employ the very language that proclaims the death of God. At this point, a great step forward has been taken by biblical scholarship, for the historical consciousness is not simply a sign of Western decadence as Nietzsche believed; it has been a primary means of willing the death of God, of collapsing transcendence into immanence, of realizing a new and awesome human autonomy. When the biblical scholar arrived at an historical understanding of the eschatological foundation of Jesus' proclamation of the Kingdom of God, he brought to an end the contemporary relevance of the biblical form of Jesus' message. No longer could the original form of the Gospel be consigned to the province of "faith," therefore it must be reduced to the level of "myth." Fundamentally, true biblical scholarship is demythologizing. The time has passed when we could live in the illusion that biblical scholarship is scientific and hence non-theological. In a theological sense, the very fact that it is "scientific" means that historical scholarship is Faustian, for to "know" scientifically means to dissolve the ground of faith, and thus to will the death of God. A true instinct led Barth to stand aside from an historical understanding of the Bible, but a deeper instinct will lead theology to say no to Barth. Even at the terrible price of the dissolution of all which theology once knew as faith, it cannot reject the destiny which awaits it.

A theology that is open to the future must first exist in the present, not a present which is an extension of the past, but a present which is a culmination of the past, and hence for us a present which is a moment of vacuity and meaninglessness. Dialectically, the very emptiness of the American present stands witness to its integral relation to a vanished past; just as the almost inevitable tendency of the European thinker to exist in the past demonstrates all too convincingly his refusal of an uprooted present. Nietzsche, who is a true prophet insofar as he speaks out of the depths of our destiny, teaches that authentic human existence is existence in the "here" and "now," in the present moment. *"In jedem Nu beginnt das Sein"* (*Zarathustra III*) is at once a portrait of our *Sein* and a call to true *Existenz*. Yes, we know that our existence (Heidegger's *Dasein* and Sartre's *pour soi*) is chaos, nothingness and despair; but we must not flee it either by clinging to a lost moment of the past or by leaping to a hopelessly transcendent eternity. We are called to accept our actual moment of existence, and to accept it by *willing* it. To refuse to will our destiny is finally to refuse both our identity and our existence. Lament as we may both the shallowness and the barbarism of life in America, we must confess that America exists in the present. Depth is absent here, and so likewise is real power, but the present is at hand, and with its advent has disappeared every form of depth and power that is rooted in the past. To the sophisticated European, America must appear as a desert, a desert shorn of the vegetation of history. But a desert can also be a gateway to the future. Ascetic virtues can arise from the nausea and the *ennui* of life in the desert; a new ascetic may arise whose very weakness will give him the strength to say no to history. If our destiny is truly one of chaos, or if we must pass through chaos to reach our destiny, then we must abandon completely the cosmos of the past.

There is some evidence to suggest the possibility that American theology is now living in the present. First of all, there is very little theology in America today: dogmatic theology has virtually disappeared, biblical scholarship is largely archeological and philological, church history barely maintains its existence as a discipline; and, in terms of German influences, Bultmann has replaced Barth as the guiding light of the younger theologians. By extending and deepening a heritage from liberal Protestantism, the American theologian is now opening himself to the logician and the philosopher, the psychiatrist and the psychoanalyst, the literary critic and the social scientist. Older theologians are dismayed as they see the traditional forms of faith gradually transformed by this process, but the one conviction that would seem to be shared by all who are actively engaged in American theology today is that these older forms of faith have no relevance to the present. Unquestionably American theology is in a process of transition, and while there is little that has thus far been accomplished to give hope for the future, the very least that can be said is that there seems no possibility that American theology will once again return to the past. Indeed, many American theologians consider Barthianism as a necessary but frightful detour from the true task of theology. Thus we must not dismiss the possibility that the poverty of contemporary American theology is witness to theology's acceptance of its vocation of silence, that at last theology has accepted its sentence of death and is preparing itself for a true renewal. The new formula for theology may well reverse the old: not the goal of converging the present and the past, but rather that of seeking a convergence of the present and the future.

Certainly a theology which genuinely looks forward to the future will be free of the temptation to bind itself to a particular past, whether that of an ecclesiastical confession or of Western civilization itself. Does this mean that theology can no longer be "Christian"? Without doubt theology must abandon Christendom, and, as we have already seen, Christendom may well include all the meaning which the word "Christian" carries to our ears. An America which since Emerson has been receptive to the Vedanta, which only recently has been deeply moved by Zen Buddhism, and has been responsive to even the vague speculations of Jung and Toynbee, and initiated once again into the history of religions by Mircea Eliade, will surely refuse a Christocentrism that is less than universal. Perhaps the most prophetic religious thinker in America today is Norman O. Brown, who is attempting to bring together radical Freudianism and left-wing mysticism (the Kabala, Boehme, Blake, Taoism, and Tantrism). And it is just this challenge of seeking a universal form of faith that will lead the American theologian to cast off his German tutors, that is, the theologians, and open himself both to the religious world of the East and to the deeper sensibility of the Western present. From the East we may once more learn the meaning of the sacred, not because the sacred has never been present in Christianity, but because Christianity in our time is in a process of dissolution and transformation. Furthermore we can encounter in the East a form of the sacred which Christianity has never known, a form which is increasingly showing itself to be relevant to our situation. Again, by opening ourselves to the radically profane form of contemporary *Existenz*, we can prepare ourselves for a new reality of the Incarnation, an Incarnation that will unite the radical sacred and the radical profane, an Incarnation that will be an ultimate *coincidentia oppositorum*. Let the Christian rejoice that only Christendom has evolved a radically profane form of *Existenz*. A profane destiny may yet provide a way to return to the God who is all in all, not by returning to a moment of the past, but by meeting an epiphany of the past in the present.

Surely no one could deny that a terrible crisis is upon us. And if a crisis brings with it an occasion for the deepest kind of creativity, it is nonetheless fraught with danger. The religious danger of our time is Gnosticism, a danger so elusive that it is impossible to define or circumscribe it. However, Nietzsche's idea of *ressentiment* can teach us a great deal about Gnosticism. For the one universal quality of all forms of true Gnosticism is a profound hatred of the world and of existence in the world. Gnosticism is a world-opposing form of faith in quest of a salvation that can be reached not by an eschatological reversal of the world or by a mystical dissolution and transformation of the world but only by the most radical kind of world-negation. Only one attitude to the world is open to the Gnostic: negation. Nor can this world-negation be dialectical. It can be nothing less than simple, ruthless, ultimate negation. To the man who is faced with the emptiness, the vacuity, and the terror of our time, Gnosticism must present the supreme temptation. Yet the man who says no to our historical present, who refuses the existence about and within him, who sets himself against our common destiny, and yet seeks release in a timeless or pre-temporal moment, a moment or "eternity" having no relation, or only a negative relation, to the present moment, is succumbing to the Gnostic danger. Moreover, in our situation, a faith which nostalgically seeks an historical past, particularly a past having no integral relation to our present, cannot escape the charge of Gnosticism. For a total refusal of our actual existence, of our destiny, can only be grounded in a Gnostic negation of the world about us. Of course, dialectical faith, whether in its Eastern or its Western, its mystical or its eschatological form, negates history. But as its negation of history is grounded in an affirmation of the present, a dialectical mode of faith can never dissociate negation and affirmation. Hence it can never know the Gnostic attitude of simple world-negation.

A contemporary form of faith is therefore called to a dialectical vocation. It can only be open to the present by negating the past. Indeed, its acceptance of the present demands an acceptance of the death of God, a *willing* of the death of God. Apart from a free acceptance of the death of God there lies no way to our profane present. From one point of view, the Christian now lives in the curse and judgment of existence in a Godless world. However, from another perspective, the very profane *Existenz* which our destiny has unveiled may yet prove to be a path to a universal form of faith. The very fact that our present is so detached from its past, from Christendom, with its corollary that an acceptance of the present demands a negation of Christendom, of the Christian God, can mean that the horizon of our present will open into a future epiphany of faith that will draw *all* things into itself. Never before has Christianity been called upon to assume a universal form, but, paradoxically, now that the Christian world has collapsed, the moment has arrived for faith to open itself to the full meaning and reality of the world. If the Word is to become flesh in our world, it must fully and finally become "flesh," become profane, and therefore it must negate all those forms of the Incarnation which effected a non-dialectical compromise between "flesh" and "Spirit." A Word that truly becomes "flesh" will no longer be "Spirit," just as a "flesh" that is transfigured by "Spirit" will no longer be "flesh." As Kierkegaard saw so deeply, faith in the Incarnation is faith in the truly absurd. Therefore the only adequate language for the Incarnation is the language of paradox, of the deepest paradox, which may well mean that it is only the language of the radical profane that can give witness to the fullest advent of the Incarnation. When faith is open to the most terrible darkness, it will be receptive to the most redemptive light. What can the Christian fear of darkness, when he knows that Christ has conquered darkness, that God will be all in all?

T. J. J. A.

Dr. J. Edward Dirks of The Christian Scholar *asked that I prepare a survey of what is going on in theology, and* "The Death of God Theologies Today" *was the result. Written in late 1963, it appeared in 1965, and can serve as a programmatic essay and introduction to the "movement" in its earliest stages.* W. H.

The Death of God Theologies Today

Complacencies of the peignoir, and late
Coffee and oranges in a sunny chair,
And the green freedom of a cockatoo
Upon a rug mingle to dissipate
The holy hush of ancient sacrifice.
She dreams a little, and she feels the dark
Encroachment of that old catastrophe....

What is divinity if it can come
Only in silent shadows and in dreams?
Shall she not find in comforts of the sun,
In pungent fruit and bright, green wings, or else
In any balm of beauty of the earth,
Things to be cherished like the thought of heaven?
Divinity must live within herself....

WALLACE STEVENS, "Sunday Morning"

We have been aware for some time that modern atheism has become a subject of special theological concern to Christians, but only recently has it moved so close to the center of theology and faith itself. The British publication of Bishop Robinson's *Honest to God* partly created and partly released forces that may well be coming together into a new theological movement in that country.[1] And there is an American counterpart to this

[1] Ronald Gregor Smith's *The New Man* (1956) was perhaps the first piece of secular theology in the British tradition. In the debate over *Honest to God* the most significant representatives of the "radical theology" come from a group of laymen which includes scientists like John Wren Lewis and James Mark, and journalists like Monica Furlong and Christopher Driver. Mark's material in the Theological Colleges Department (SCM) brochure "The Death of the Church" is worth study.

British movement, though it goes back in time a bit before *Honest to God*. This American movement is the death of God theology. It is a movement, though until quite recently there was no communication between the participants. But they have begun to talk to each other and to discover that there are a handful of people here and there who one day may all contribute to a common theological style. Right now, the American death of God movement seems to be more radical than the British "radicals," more radical on each of the three main points of *Honest to God*—God, ethics and the church. To the death of God theologian, Robinson is far too confident about the possibility of God-language. To use Paul van Buren's terms, Robinson is perfectly right to reject objectified theism, but he is wrong to think that his non-objectified theism is any more satisfactory. Van Buren would claim that modern philosophy has done away with both possibilities.

But unlike many American theologians, the death of God people do not patronize *Honest to God*. They take its publication as an important event in the life of the church, and they note particularly its enthusiastic reception by the laity as a sign that they may have a theological vocation in the church after all, in spite of the fact that their writing has up to now given more ecclesiastical offense than they expected. In any case, the purpose here is not to study the British radicals but to describe this American theological tradition and to ask under what conditions it might become part of the very lively theological discussion going on right now in this country.[2]

What is meant by the phrase "death of God"? My colleague, Thomas Altizer, likes to say, for example, that the death of God is an historical event, that it has happened in our time and that

[2] In a recent series of lectures (entitled "Is God Dead?" and "God Is Not Dead.") published in *The Voice* (Crozier Theological Seminary), Dr. Langdon Gilkey of the University of Chicago has made a provisional exposition and criticism of this theological position. Gilkey is in a kind of horrified sympathy with the death of God theology, and he has made a number of shrewd criticisms and raised some important questions.

we should welcome, even will it, not shrink from it.[3] But if we call it an event, it is so in a special or odd sense, for it has not been experienced in any regular or ordinary way. The reference to Nietzsche's *Gay Science* is deliberate, and perhaps we ought to have the relevant material before us.

The Madman.—Have you ever heard of the madman who on a bright morning lighted a lantern and ran to the market-place calling out unceasingly: "I seek God! I seek God!"—As there were many people standing about who did not believe in God, he caused a great deal of amusement. Why! is he lost? said one. Has he strayed away like a child? said another. Or does he keep himself hidden? Is he afraid of us? Has he taken a sea-voyage? Has he emigrated?—the people cried out laughingly, all in a hubbub. The insane man jumped into their midst and transfixed them with his glances. "Where is God gone?" he called out. "I mean to tell you! *We have killed him,*—you and I! We are all his murderers! But how have we done it? How were we able to drink up the sea? Who gave us the sponge to wipe away the whole horizon? What did we do when we loosened this earth from its sun? Whither does it now move? Whither do we move?

Away from all suns? Do we not dash on unceasingly? Backwards, sideways, forwards, in all directions? Is there still an above and below? Do we not stray, as through infinite nothing-

---

[3] In citing Altizer I am by no means suggesting that he is alone in his emphasis. Gabriel Vahanian of Syracuse has done some important work in his *The Death of God* and *Wait Without Idols,* in "Beyond the Death of God," *Dialog,* Autumn, 1962, and in "The Future of Christianity in a Post-Christian Era," *The Centennial Review,* Spring, 1964. John Cobb of Claremont has an excellent descriptive article, by no means in sympathy with the movement, in "From Crisis Theology to the Post-Modern World," *The Centennial Review,* Spring, 1964. Mention should also be made of the work of the New Testament scholars Robert Funk and Edward Hobbs; of the work of the Jewish scholar Richard L. Rubenstein, especially his excellent "Person and Myth in the Judaeo-Christian Encounter," *The Christian Scholar,* Winter, 1963. Rudolf Bultmann himself has written, not perhaps at his best, on this tradition in "Der Gottesgedanke und der moderne Mensch," *Zeitschrift für Theologie und Kirche,* December, 1963. (ET. in *Translating Theology into The Modern Age,* Harper, Torchbooks, 1965.)

ness? Does not empty space breathe upon us? Has it not become colder? Does not night come on continually, darker and darker? Shall we not have to light lanterns in the morning? Do we not hear the noise of the grave-diggers who are burying God? Do we not smell the divine putrefaction?—for even gods putrefy! God is dead! God remains dead! And we have killed him! How shall we console ourselves, the most murderous of all murderers? The holiest and the mightiest that the world has hitherto possessed, has bled to death under our knife,—who will wipe the blood from us? With what water could we cleanse ourselves? What lustrums, what sacred games shall we have to devise? Is not the magnitude of this deed too great for us? Shall we not ourselves have to become Gods, merely to seem worthy of it? There never was a greater event,—and on account of it, all who are born after us belong to a higher history than any history hitherto!"—Here the madman was silent and looked again at his hearers; they also were silent and looked at him in surprise. At last he threw his lantern on the ground, so that it broke in pieces and was extinguished. "I come too early," he then said, "I am not yet at the right time. This prodigious event is still on its way, and is travelling,—it has not yet reached men's ears. Lightning and thunder need time, the light of the stars needs time, deeds need time, even after they are done, to be seen and heard. This deed is as yet further from them than the furthest star,—*and yet they have done it!*" It is further stated that the madman made his way into different churches on the same day, and there intoned his *Requiem aeternam deo*. When led out and called to account, he always gave the reply: "What are these churches now, if they are not the tombs and monuments of God?" . . .[4]

What does it mean to say that God is dead? Is this any more than a rather romantic way of pointing to the traditional difficulty of speaking about the holy God in human terms? Is it any more than a warning against all idols, all divinities fashioned out of human need, human ideologies? Does it perhaps not just mean that "existence is not an appropriate word to

[4] No. 125. An important recent study of Nietzsche which places "the death of God" at the center of his thought can be found in Erich Heller, "The Importance of Nietzsche," *Encounter*, April, 1964.

ascribe to God, that therefore he cannot be said to exist, and he is in that sense dead"? It surely means all this, and more. The hypothetical meanings suggested still all lie within the safe boundaries of the neo-orthodox or biblical-theology tradition, and the death of God group wants clearly to break away from that. It used to live rather comfortably there, and does so no longer.[5] Perhaps we can put it this way; the neo-orthodox reconstruction of the Christian doctrine of revelation seems to have broken down for some. It used to be possible to say: we cannot know God but he has made himself known to us, and at that point analogies from the world of personal relations would enter the scene and help us. But somehow, the situation has deteriorated; as before, we cannot know, but now it seems that he does not make himself known, even as enemy. This is more than the old protest against natural theology or metaphysics; more than the usual assurance that before the holy God all our language gets broken and diffracted into paradox. It

[5] Dr. Gilkey has clearly observed the senses in which the death of God theology is not a return to liberalism and has a very interesting remark on the connections between it and neo-orthodoxy:

> From Barth this movement has accepted the radical separation of the divine and the secular, of God and ordinary experience, and so of theological language and philosophy; and it approves his further separation of Christianity and religion, and the consequent centering of all theological and religious concerns solely on Jesus Christ. From Tillich it has accepted the campaign against theism, and against personalist and mythological language about God. From Bultmann it has absorbed the polemic against ancient "mythological" categories in theology, which polemic needed only to be enlarged to include biblical-kerygmatic as well as objective-interventionist theological language about God to become very radical indeed. It also agrees with Bultmann that objective ontological and dogmatic language about God is impossible, with the consequence that theological language is reduced to language about the figure of Jesus Christ and about man's self-understanding.

This is a very shrewd observation by one who probably knows as much about what is really happening in American theology today as anybody. This passage shows the connections between the death of God movement and some of the left-wing Bultmannians who have not advanced to metaphysics.

is really that we do not know, do not adore, do not possess, do not believe in God. It is not just that a capacity has dried up within us; we do not take all this as merely a statement about our frail psyches, we take it as a statement about the nature of the world and we try to convince others. God is dead. We are not talking about the absence of the experience of God, but about the experience of the absence of God.[6] Yet the death of God theologians claim to be theologians, to be Christians, to be speaking out of a community to a community. They do not grant that their view is really a complicated sort of atheism dressed in a new spring bonnet. Let us look more carefully at their work.

I

Thomas Altizer's book, *Mircea Eliade and the Dialectic of the Sacred*, was published late in 1963 and has so far attracted very little attention. In the book Altizer has not decided whether to do a book on Eliade (to whom he owes a profound debt) or an original piece of theological exposition. He comes up with a little of both, and the result is not structurally satisfactory. But it is a brilliant book in many ways and an important piece of material in the movement.

Altizer begins by declaring that his basic presupposition is the death of God in our history, for us, now. A theology of the word can ignore this death, he says, but only by keeping the word quite untouched by the reality of modern existence. So Altizer lays out the problems raised for him by the death of God in terms of the sacred and the profane, and this enables him to make interesting use of Eliade's studies of the meaning of the sacred in archaic and modern religion. Altizer's question becomes, then, how to recover that connection with the sacred that modern men have lost. He grants that gnosticism, the negation of the profane, is a powerful temptation at this point, and

---

[6] Thus, we are moving in quite a different direction from the rather vague remark by Martin Heidegger: "the phrase 'God is dead' means that the supersensible world is without effective force." *Holzwege,* Frankfurt, Klostermann, 1957, p. 200.

he tries very hard to reject it. We must not, he says, seek for the sacred by saying "no" to the radical profanity of our age, but by saying "yes" to it. Thus, he writes, "the task of the theologian becomes the paradoxical one of unveiling religious meaning in a world that is bathed in the darkness of God's absence."

This statement suggests that Altizer, like Nietzsche, finds it a painful thing to have to affirm the death of God, and it is clear that he wishes things were otherwise. But he refuses to follow Eliade's tempting advice to return to some sort of pre-cosmic primitivism and to recover the sacred in the way archaic religion did. How does the sacred become a possibility for a man who refuses to think himself out of his radically profane contemporary existence, who refuses in other words to archaize himself, with Eliade into primitivism or with Barth into the strange new world of the Bible?

Apparently the answer comes in Altizer's use of the Kierke-gaardian idea of dialectic, or—what comes to the same thing—in his reading of Eliade's version of the myth of the coinci-dence of opposites. This means that affirming something passionately enough—in this case the full reality of the profane, secular, worldly character of modern life—will somehow de-liver to the seeker the opposite, the sacred, as a gift he does not deserve. At times, Altizer walks very close to the gnostic nay-sayer whose danger he ordinarily perceives. His interest in the religious writing, such as it is, of Norman O. Brown is a sign of his own religious-gnostic temptations. Brown not only mounts an undialectical Freudian attack on the profane and the secular, he sees both history and ordinary genital sexuality as needing to be radically spiritualized and tran-scended. His religious vision, both at the end of *Life Against Death* and in his more recent thought, is mystical, spiritual and apocalyptic. This temptation is not a persistent one in Altizer, and in one important section of his book he makes the most ungnostic remark that the sacred will be born only when Western man combines a willing acceptance of the profane with a desire to change it.

For the most part Altizer prefers mystical to ethical language in solving the problem of the death of God, or, as he puts it, in mapping out the way from the profane to the sacred. This combination of Kierkegaard and Eliade makes rather rough reading, but his position at the end is a relatively simple one. Here is an important summary statement of his views:

> If theology must now accept a dialectical vocation, it must learn the full meaning of Yes-saying and No-saying; it must sense the possibility of a Yes which can become a No, and of a No which can become a Yes; in short, it must look forward to a dialectical *coincidentia oppositorum.* Let theology rejoice that faith is once again a "scandal," and not simply a moral scandal, an offense to man's pride and righteousness, but, far more deeply, an ontological scandal; for eschatological faith is directed against the deepest reality of what we know as history and the cosmos. Through Nietzsche's vision of Eternal Recurrence we can sense the ecstatic liberation that can be occasioned by the collapse of the transcendence of Being, by the death of God . . . and, from Nietzsche's portrait of Jesus, theology must learn of the power of an eschatological faith that can liberate the believer from what to the contemporary sensibility is the inescapable reality of history. But liberation must finally be effected by affirmation. . . .*

This is an ebullient, crotchety statement, full of linguistic and logical difficulties. Some of Altizer's Kierkegaardian or Nietzschean or gnostic uneasiness in the presence of the vulgar historical can be seen in it. But it is also powerful and poetic, with a good deal of the radical eschatological message of the New Testament in it, calling men out of the world into the presence of Jesus.

For Altizer men do not solve the problem of the death of God by following Jesus, but, it seems, by being liberated from history by him. In spite of his insight that ethics (or transforming the profane) can be a real way of handling the problem of the ambiguity of the profane realm, Altizer ultimately prefers the categories of neither Christology nor ethics but of

---

* See "Theology and the Death of God," in this volume, pp. 95-111.

mysticism. Thus his vision, beginning with man accepting, affirming, even willing the death of God in a radical sense, ends with man willing to participate in the utter desolation of the secular or the profane, willing to undergo the discipline of darkness, the dark night of the soul (here Altizer's affinity with the religious existentialists, who may not have God but who don't at all like not having him, is clearest), while the possibility of a new epiphany of the sacred, a rebirth of the possibility of having God once more is awaited. Sometimes Altizer would have us wait quietly without terror; more often it seems he would have us attack the profane world with a kind of terrible hostility so that it might give up its sacred secret.

Altizer's vision is an exciting one, logically imprecise, calculated to make empiricists weep, but imaginatively and religiously it is both sophisticated and powerful.[7]

II

The work of Paul van Buren says something about the rather strange sense of community that one finds in the death of God group that two such different personalities as van Buren and Altizer could have a common theological vocation. Altizer is all *élan*, wildness, excessive generalization, brimming with col-

[7] In "Word and History," in this volume, pp. 121-139, Altizer makes one point not found so strongly in his other writings, and it is a point that the death of God writers tend to have in common. It is that America has a theological vocation today that is likely to be quite separate from the European experience. The group has a strong sense of being in a particular place, urban America, and at a particular time; born in the twenties, just old enough (usually) to get into World War II, products of the affluent society, very conscious of being white. This intense, and perhaps overemphasized Americanism, should not be dismissed as chauvinism, nor should it be passed off as some sort of guilt for having loved Barth or Bultmann too much. All of us have drawn from many non-American sources, not the least important of which is the later Bonhoeffer. But this special sense of a vocation to America should be noted, and it is no doubt part of the whole post-existentialist self-consciousness so characteristic of the group.

See the important article by Robert Funk, "Colloquium on Hermeneutics," *Theology Today*, October, 1964.

orful, flamboyant, and emotive language. Van Buren is ordered, precise, cool. While he has certainly moved beyond the position of his book, it is in fact his book, *The Secular Meaning of the Gospel*, that has placed him firmly in the death of God camp, and we must briefly recall its major emphases.

Van Buren begins by citing Bonhoeffer's plea for a non-religious interpretation of the Gospel, appropriate to the world come of age. The title of his book reflects this Bonhoefferean concern, though the book as a whole does not, and the Bonhoeffer introduction is really extraneous to his argument.

He next moves on to a consideration of the method he proposes for his non-religious theology, and it turns out to be a certain species of linguistic analysis, but the theological context within which van Buren puts his method to work is, after all, that created by Bultmann and his demythologizing project, and van Buren very clearly sees the sense in which Bultmann, taken seriously, means the end of the rhetoric of neo-orthodoxy and the so-called biblical theology.

> The mythological view of the world has gone, and with it went the possibility of speaking seriously of a *Heilsgeschichte:* a historical "drama of salvation," in which God is said to have acted at a certain time in this world to change the state of human affairs.

He rejects Barth who is described as forfeiting the world as we live in it today (precisely the reason for Altizer's rejection of the theologies of the word), and he rejects also the left-wing Bultmannians who have, he justly remarks, given up the historical basis of faith for an idea of authentic existence. In van Buren's debate with a left-wing Bultmannian like Schubert Ogden we can see what he is after. What he attacks in Ogden is the belief that there is *any* trustworthy language about God at all, either analogical language or retranslations such as the odd one Ogden uses: God as "experienced non-objective reality."

Van Buren is inclined to assume that analytical philosophy has made all language about God impossible. He is not talking about the deterioration of our experience of God, and he is not talking about the loss of the sacred. He is talking about words, and how hard it is to find the right ones. "Simple literal theism" is out, he says, but so is the kind of sophisticated and qualified non-objective theism that he finds in Ogden, Tillich, Karl Jaspers, and that he ought to find in Bishop Robinson.

It is not necessary to raise the question as to whether van Buren is guilty of taking this philosophical tradition too seriously, of receiving the impressive blows it is able to deliver with too radical a retreat. The fact remains that he has set about to do his theological work without God. There is something remaining in the vacated space, and perhaps the idea of one's historical perspective or point of view can be used to rebuild the old notion of faith as *assensus* and *fiducia* before God. Perhaps. But apart from this, we do without God and hold to Jesus of Nazareth.

Thus, the urban and methodologically scrupulous van Buren joins hands with Altizer the ecstatic and complex proclaimer of the death of God. The tone of voice is quite different; indeed the languages are not the same, but the meaning is unmistakable in both: God is dead. For Altizer the disappearance of the sacred is a sort of cosmic event; for van Buren it can be more precisely described: the rise of technology and modern science, the need in our thinking to stick pretty close to what we can experience in ordinary ways. Both are referring to something that has happened to them, not to someone else or to modern man in some generalized sense, and they are willing to admit it.

Altizer comes finally to depend on mystical categories to deal with the death of God, to save himself from undialectical atheism. Van Buren is too loyal an erstwhile Barthian to want to use mystical categories: for him ethical terms will do. When the theisms have gone, literal or fancy, as they must, and after faith has been Ramseyed and Hared, Christianity still stands as an ethic, public and private, and its character is largely derived from the sovereign freedom of Jesus the Lord. The Christian without God is a waiting man for Altizer, daring to descend into the darkness, grappling with all that is profane to wrest from it its potential sacral power. The Christian without God for van Buren is Jesus' man, perfectly free lord of all, subject to none.[8]

Altizer and van Buren, thus, may be said to share a common vision which we have been calling the death of God, though this actual phrase is doubtless more congenial to the fiery Altizer than to the lucid van Buren. Both men, furthermore, deny that this vision disqualifies them as religious or Christian men. It may cripple, it may weaken or threaten, but they are both inside the circle. And each uses a different strategy to deal with the problem raised by the vision. Altizer, as we have seen, uses images from the world of mysticism: waiting, darkness, a new epiphany, the dialectic of opposites. Van Buren does without and does not really need God, preferring to point to Jesus as a way of standing before the neighbor. We will meet later in the book this distinction between mysticism

[8] The contemporary religious philosopher closest to van Buren, in mood at least, is Alasdair MacIntyre in "God and the Theologians," *Encounter*, September, 1963, an extended review of *Honest to God*, a valedictory to the Christian faith, and an interesting and confused piece of work. His chief point is that all three of Robinson's theologians, Bonhoeffer, Bultmann and Tillich, are atheists, which he apparently defines as those rejecting literal objectifiable theism. But this is to swallow the apologetic strategy of Karl Barth without a murmur. Barth has always loved to dangle the threatening figure of Feuerbach before anyone interested in the self, modern man, or despair, and to say, in effect, "Look out, gentlemen; if you leave my protection and go down the slippery path towards Bultmann or Tillich you will be unable to stop until you arrive at Feuerbach, who was at least honest in his atheism." MacIntyre has apparently been beguiled by this device. Using the same tools as van Buren, he has declared for overt atheism rather than the death of God, and also, with Feuerbach, has chosen the historical fate of man and his freedom in this world, to salvation and the next. It is, incidentally, unfortunate that modern Protestants have trusted Barth as an interpreter of Feuerbach. Robert Tucker has pointed out (*Philosophy and Myth in Karl Marx*, p. 93) that Feuerbach mistakenly assumed that his foe, Christianity, was identical with Hegelianism. Since he was unable to see how deeply anti-Christian Hegelianism really was, his inversion of Christianity was really an inversion of Hegelian Christianity and thus, to say the least, more Christian in substance than Hegelianism ever was.

and a Christological ethic as different ways of living in the time of the death of God.

III

My own point of view belongs in this general tradition. If Altizer begins with the cosmic event of the disappearance of the sacred, and if van Buren begins with the language problem, my starting point may be said to have two parts, one negative, the other positive.

The negative part is the perception, already referred to, of the deterioration of the portrait of the God-man relation as found in biblical theology and the neo-orthodox tradition. This theological tradition was able to portray a striking and even heroic faith, a sort of holding on by the fingernails to the cliff of faith, a standing terrified before the enemy-God, present to man as terror or threat, comforting only in that he kept us from the worse terrors of life without him. This God, we used to say, will never let us go. But he has, or we have him, or something, and in any case this whole picture has lost its power to persuade some in our time.

But our negations are never very important or interesting. There is a positive affirmation or starting point by which I enter into the country inhabited by the death of God settlers. It has to do with the problem of the Reformation or being a Protestant today. At the end of the last century the Reformation was interpreted as a victory for the autonomous religious personality, freed from the tyranny of hierarchy and institution, while man's relation to God was described as unmediated and available to all. This is what the Reformation means, for example, in A. von Harnack's *What is Christianity?* It was characteristic of liberal Protestantism as a whole, and it achieves its symbolic expression in Luther, standing alone at Worms, refusing to go against his conscience.

As the century wore on, and wars, depressions, bombs and anxieties came our way, we found ourselves seeing the Reformation in a new light. The old approach was not wrong, it was just that the new approach fitted our experience better.

In this new approach, which we might call yesterday's under-standing of the Reformation, the central fact was not the autonomous religious personality; it was the theological dis-covery of the righteous God. In that portion of our century when men and nations knew trouble, sin and guilt, we needed to receive this theological truth of the Reformation, just as earlier the psychological truth needed to be heard. Thus, we learned to say that the Reformation was a theological event. It centered in Luther's discovery of the meaning of justification or forgiveness, and its symbol proved to be Luther, storming about his room in Wittenberg, cursing the God who demands righteousness of men.

Today we may need to look at the Reformation in a third sense, no more or less true than the earlier approaches, but perhaps needing special emphasis just now and fitting new experiences in both church and world. This approach is more ethical than psychological or theological, and its focus is not on the free personality or on justification by faith, but on the movement from the cloister to the world. Of course, there is no specific event in Luther's life that can be so described, but the movement is there in his life nonetheless, and it is a move-ment we need to study. From cloister to world means from church, from place of protection and security, of order and beauty, to the bustling middle-class world of the new university, of politics, princes and peasants. Far more important than any particular ethical teaching of Luther is this fundamental ethical movement. Here I touch some of Altizer's concerns, but I am not as anxious to recover the sacred, since I am starting with a definition of Protestantism as a movement away from the sacred place.

This view of the Reformation, along with my preliminary negative comment, does allow a kind of picture of faith. It is not, this time, holding on by the fingernails, and it is not a terror-struck confession before the enemy God. It is not even a means of apprehending God at all. This faith is more like a place, a being with or standing beside the neighbor. Faith has almost collapsed into love, and the Protestant is no longer defined as the forgiven sinner, the *simul justus et peccator*, but as the one beside the neighbor, beside the enemy, at the disposal of the man in need. The connection between holding to the neighbor and holding to Jesus will be dealt with in a moment.

Here I reflect the thought of the later Bonhoeffer more than either van Buren or Altizer wants or needs to. My Protestant has no God, has no faith in God, and affirms both the death of God and the death of all the forms of theism. Even so, he is not primarily a man of negation, for if there is a movement away from God and religion, there is the more important movement into, for, toward the world, worldly life, and the neighbor as the bearer of the worldly Jesus. We must look more carefully at these two movements: toward the world and away from religion.

IV

We need to be very careful in how we put this Protestant "yes" to the world. It is not the same kind of "yes" that one finds in that tradition of theology of culture today that makes use of the world as illustrations for its doctrines of sin and redemption. This "yes" is also in considerable tension with a number of themes in modern literature. Recently, Lionel Trilling called attention to Thomas Mann's remark that all his work was an effort to free himself from the middle class, and to this Trilling added the comment that all truly modern literature can be so described. Indeed, he goes on, modern literature is not only asking for a freedom from the middle class, but from society itself. It is this conception of the modern, I am saying, that should be opposed by the Protestant. Who are the characteristically modern writers in this sense I am criticising? Any such list would surely include Henry James, Eliot, Yeats, Pound, Joyce, Lawrence, Kafka, Faulkner, Beckett. Is it possible to affirm the value of the technological revolution, the legitimacy of the hopes and claims of the dispossessed, most of all, of the moral centrality of the Negro revolution in America today—is it possible to affirm all these values and still to live comfortably in the modern world as these writers portray it? Surely not, in some important senses.

To say there is something in the essence of Protestantism itself that drives us into the world is not to say that we are driven to the world of these "modern" writers. But in many ways it is into the world they reject—to the world of technology, power, money, sex, culture, race, poverty and the city—that we are driven. Lawrence's protest against the mechanization of life now seems a bit archaic and piquant, and his aristocratic hostility to the democratic ethos of Christianity is rather more than piquant, it is irrelevant and false. In a way, I am describing not a move away from Puritanism, but a move to it, and to the middle class and to the city. Perhaps the time has come when Protestants no longer need to make ritual acts of hostility to Puritanism, moralism, and to all the hypocrisies and prohibitions of middle-class culture. The chronicle of middle-class hypocrisy may well be complete, with no more work on it necessary. There are those in our world today who would like to be a little closer to the securities of middle-class existence so they too might become free to criticize them, and who must indeed be granted political, economic, and psychological admission to that world. Attacks on the silliness of middle-class morality have almost always had an a-political character, and it is to that element in the modern sensibility that the Protestant takes exception. Thus the worldliness affirmed by Protestanism has a post-modern, pro-bourgeois, urban and political character. This may mean a loosening of the ties between the Protestant intellectual and avant-garde modernism and it might even mean the start of some interesting work in the shaping of a contemporary radical ethic.

The Protestant protest against religion is related to, but it must not be confused with, this affirmation of the world. (Both are clearly implied by our formula, from church to world.) Assertions that Protestantism is against religion, or that Christianity or revelation is an attack on religion, have, of course, been with us for a considerable time now, and nearly everybody has had a word to say on the subject. Karl Barth's long discussion in *Church Dogmatics* I/2 has had a massive and perhaps undeserved influence. Barth defines religion, in his attack on it, as something like man's arrogant and grasping attempt to become God, so it is hard to see what all the posturing is about. If by definition religion equals sin, and you then say revelation ought to be against religion, you may bring some delight to careless readers, but you have not forwarded theological clarity very much.

More immediate in influence, of course, is the plea for a religionless Christianity in the prison letters of Bonhoeffer. We really don't know what Bonhoeffer meant by religion, and our modern study of the problem of religionlessness must be carried on quite independent of the task, probably fruitless, of establishing just what Bonhoeffer meant.

There are two schools of interpretation of Protestant religionlessness. In the moderate, Honest-to-God, ecclesiastical school of interpretation, religion generally means "religious activities" like liturgy, counselling, going to church, saying your prayers. To be religionless in this sense is to affirm that the way we have done these things in the past may not be the only way, or may not be worth doing at all, and that radical experiments ought to be attempted in the forms of the church and ministry. Bishop Robinson's lectures on "The New Reformation" delivered in America in the spring of 1964 are an able presentation of this moderate radicalism. A good deal of the material out of New York, Geneva, and the denominational headquarters on the church and ministry reflects this promising line, and a good many religious sociologists and radical religious leaders on the race issue tend to use Bonhoeffer and religionlessness in this way.

This is an important trend, and we need more and not less experimentation on these matters of the ministry, for we are well into the opening phase of the breakdown of organized religion in American life, well beyond the time when ecumenical dialogues or denominational mergers can be expected to arrest the breakdown.

The religionlessness I wish to defend, however, is not of this practical type. At no point is the later Bonhoeffer of greater importance to the death of God theology than in helping us work out a truly theological understanding of the problem of religionlessness. I take religion to mean not man's arrogant grasping for God (Barth) and not assorted Sabbath activities usually performed by ordained males (the moderate radicals), but any system of thought or action in which God or the gods serve as fulfiller of needs or solver of problems. Thus I assert with Bonhoeffer the breakdown of the religious *a priori* and the coming of age of man.

The breakdown of the religious *a priori* means that there is no way, ontological, cultural or psychological, to locate a part of the self or a part of human experience that needs God. There is no God-shaped blank within man. Man's heart may or may not be restless until it rests in God. It is not necessarily so. God is not in the realm of the necessary at all; he is not necessary being, he is not necessary to avoid despair or self-righteousness. He is one of the possibles in a radically pluralistic spiritual and intellectual milieu.

This is just what man's coming of age is taken to mean. It is not true to say, with Luther, *entweder Gott oder Abgott*. It is not true to say, with Ingmar Bergman, "Without God, life is an outrageous terror." It is not true to say that there are certain areas, problems, dimensions to life today that can only be faced, solved, illumined, dealt with, by a religious perspective.

Religion is to be defined as the assumption in theology, preaching, apologetics, evangelism, counselling, that man needs God, and that there are certain things that God alone can do for him. I am denying that religion is necessary and saying that the movement from the church to the world that we have taken as definitive of Protestantism not only permits but requires this denial. To assert that we are men moving from cloister to world, church to world, to say that we are secular men, is to say that we do not ask God to do for us what the world is qualified to do. Really to travel along this road means that we trust the world, not God, to be our need fulfiller and problem solver, and God, if he is to be for us at all, must come in some other role.

This combination of a certain kind of God-rejection with a certain kind of world-affirmation is the point where I join the death of God movement. What distinguishes this position from ordinary Feuerbachian atheism? Earlier we distinguished between mysticism and Christological ethics as ways of handling the historical experience of the death of God. Both of these responses are valid and useful, and in answering the question about atheism I would like to propose my version of them.

I am in full sympathy with much of the mystical imagery used by Altizer, perhaps most of all with the idea of "waiting." There is an element of expectation, even hope, that removes my position from classical atheisms and that even removes from it a large amount of anguish and gloom. In addition to the idea of waiting for God, I am interested in the search for a language that does not depend on need or problem. Perhaps the Augustinian distinction between *frui* and *uti* will prove to be helpful. If God is not needed, if it is to the world and not God that we repair for our needs and problems, then perhaps we may come to see that he is to be enjoyed and delighted in. Part of the meaning of waiting for God is found in this attempt to understand what delighting in him might mean.

To the valid theme of the Christological ethic worked out by van Buren add the emphasis on Protestant worldliness both as an interpretation of the Reformation and as an attack on certain forms of modern sensibility.

By way of a provisional summary: the death of God must be affirmed; the confidence with which we thought we could speak of God is gone, and our faith, belief, experience of him are very poor things indeed. Along with this goes a sharp attack on religion which we have defined as any system using God to meet a need or to solve a problem, even the problem of not having a God. Our waiting for God, our godlessness, is partly a search for a language and a style by which we might be enabled to stand before him once again, delighting in his presence.

In the time of waiting we have a place to be. It is not before an altar, it is in the world, in the city, with both the needy neighbor and the enemy. This place really defines our faith, for faith and love have come together in the interim of waiting. This place, as we shall see, is not only the place for the waiting for God, it is also a way to Jesus Christ.[9]

v

It seems clear to me that American theological thought and action has been, for perhaps thirty years, in what might be called an Oedipal phase, and the time has come for it to move into its post-Oedipal situation. The hero of the new situation must no longer be Oedipus at all, but Orestes. In other terms, the post-medieval hero of the Christian consciousness has been Hamlet, and we have all made our struggle for faith in his shadow. But we must move beyond Hamlet, and the Shakespearean hero that can guide us is Prospero.

It is interesting to observe how Orestes has come to fascinate writers of widely different perspectives today. O'Neill has treated the whole saga in *Mourning Becomes Electra*. Eliot in *The Family Reunion* and Sartre in *The Flies* have each left their stamp on the Greek hero, and today even Jack Richardson in *The Prodigal* has brought Orestes into the world of modern experimental theater. In a fascinating article, "Orestes: Paradigm Hero and Central Motif of Contemporary Ego Psychology," in *The Psychoanalytic Review*, Fall, 1963, Herbert Fingarette has suggested that Orestes has the power to become the hero in the modern world of ego psychology and identity crisis. This may or may not be the case, but it is true that Orestes

[9] This combination of waiting, enjoyment and a Christological ethic brings my position close to that of Hanfried Müller, the East Berlin theologian and author of the best book to date on Bonhoeffer, *Von der Kirche zur Welt*. Müller's basic theological principle is the theology of the cross, and as he interprets this—no present experience of Incarnation or resurrection, etc.—it is close to, but not perhaps as extreme as the vision of the death of God. But to the *theologia crucis* Müller adds, and this is a real source of interest and distinguishes him from Kierkegaard, a social-political optimism which, in his case of course, is derived from Marxism. One wonders whether the Negro revolution in America may not provide a context for a similar combination of the cross and optimism. Cf. J. M. Lochman's essay on Müller, "From the Church to the World," in *New Theology No. 1.*, edited by Marty and Peerman.

can serve as a symbolic theological guide. What does this mean?

Oedipal theology today asks such questions as these: "Who is my Father? Is rebellion against the Father permissible, or must I submit? What can I love in the loveless world? Where is the true locus of authority? Is there any Father for me to love?" And it is a theology based on a sense of sin: "I am a sinner, I love my mother and I desire to kill my Father." The Oedipal believer is a man standing still and alone in a desolate place. He is looking up to the heavens, he has no eyes of flesh, only eyes of faith, and he is crying out his questions to the heavens.

Psychologically, as Fingarette shows, Oedipus stands for the individual as he moves into his central crisis of growth, as he solves the problems of his adolescence or coming of age. Orestes, on the other hand, is the individual having moved beyond this crisis. Oedipus shows us the individual's psychological bondage, Orestes shows us his freedom and struggle for harmony. Orestes, as Aeschylus portrays him, returns from exile to his royal home. He comes back to the place where his father was murdered and where his mother took up her liaison with Aegisthus, who aided her in the murder. Now grown, Orestes comes back to the Oedipal situation. He could have remained in exile, but he did not. He chose to return. Unlike Oedipus, he does not perform his acts out of fate, but out of a destiny. Unlike Oedipus, he has a direction. Orestes had made a vow to Apollo to take up his responsibility as son and heir. It is not fate, but his own free vow to Apollo that binds him. As he returns, he comes to see that he must destroy the faithless mother.

Oedipus inadvertently kills the father, while Orestes chooses to kill the corrupt mother, out of loyalty to the father. Psychologically, we are in a new world beyond the Oedipal state, and religiously we are in a new world as well. Out of loyalty to both the gods and to the memory of the murdered father, the mother must be destroyed, the mother who represents security, warmth, religion, authority, but who has become corrupt and an evil bearer of all that she is supposed to represent.

This readily points to the theological task of post-Oedipal,

Orestean theology. To be freed from the parents is to be freed from religion, the religious *a priori,* religion as necessary, God as meeter of needs and solver of problems. Orestean theology means the end of faith's preoccupation with inner conflict, of the struggle of faith, of the escape from the enemy God, of the careful confession of sin. When the believing man can thus abandon this mode of introspective self-scrutiny, "then the center of a man's existence is himself as a man among men, a man *of* the real world and not merely in it." Fingarette goes on to say:

> . . . a man of the world, in the sense here intended, is a man at last open to the world and to his fellow men as his fellows. And, although in a certain sense men's existence is the center, this does not imply, either in the play or in life, a denial of the marvelous, both holy and profane.

At the close of the Aeschylean trilogy, Athena sets Orestes free, and Apollo and Orestes leave the center of the action, and the city, the *polis,* dominates our attention at the end. Orestes has returned home in obedience to a vow, cleansed the state of the evil infecting it (which happened to be his own mother) and takes up his role as prince and ruler. The psychological interpretation of the hero refers to the need for mastering and accepting our anxiety and finding a constructive role in society. Theologically, we must also claim Orestes as our paradigmatic hero, for we too must reject the mother. Unlike Orestes, who kills the mother because of a loyalty to the father, we must kill the mother in order to discover the as yet unformed meaning of our loyalty to the father. In order to overcome the death of the father in our lives, the death of God, the mother must be abolished and we must give our devotion to the *polis,* to the city, politics and our neighbor. Waiting for God, expecting the transcendent and the marvelous, searching for a means of enjoying them, we go out into the world and the city and, working, wait there.

Thus, Protestant men, Protestant churches, and, most important here, Protestant theology, belongs in the street if it is to be truly Orestean. The academy and the temple can, for now, no longer be trusted as theological guides. Not only our action but our thought belongs with the world of the city, which in our time means power, culture, art, sex, money, the Jew, the Negro, beauty, ugliness, poverty and indifference. Thought and action both must make the move from Oedipus to Orestes, from self and anxiety and crying out to the enemy-God, to the neighbor, the city, the world.

But the movement from Oedipus to Orestes has an Elizabethan counterpart. It is also the move from Hamlet to Prospero. What does it mean to say that Hamlet-theology is at an end and that we need to discern some clues in Prospero? Hamlet-theology, like that of his spiritual ancestor Oedipus, is about authority and about the father. Is the ghost really the father, and should he be obeyed? Shall I acquiesce in his demand, even though it is for blood revenge, or shall I rebel against the father? The Hamlet theology, thus, is one in which man is largely alone, in which he is obsessed by his own and his people's rottenness, and in which he, in his solitariness, wonders about God and what God wills. If there is any action (or ethics) that emerges from such a theology, it is fairly arbitrary and does not proceed out of interior soliloquy at all, but comes rather in response to surface stimuli. To mark the end of solitariness as a theological posture, of obsessive senses of sin, of crying out to God, absent or present, is to mark the end, in Protestant circles at least, of the existentialist mood.

But to move beyond Hamlet is to come to sit before Prospero. What does this mean? The Prospero I would propose as a model is not the forgiver but the man who gives up his magic, his charismatic power, and releases Ariel. We hear him say, "this rough magic I here abjure" (V.1.50-51) and "Now my charms are all o'erthrown" (Epilogue). Prospero is the man who leaves the place of mystery and magic and returns to his Dukedom in Milan. He moves from the sacred, from magic, from religion, to the world of the city. Prospero's abjuring of magic is parallel to Orestes' killing of the faithless mother, and his return to his rightful Dukedom is parallel to Orestes' return to Argos and his princely duties.

VI

I must now attempt to draw some of these themes together, so that this death of God tradition may have as good a chance as possible of taking on a theological life of its own along with the other theological styles and visions that we are beginning to discern in this new post-existentialist, post-European period. (Professor Gilkey has listed five marks of the death of God tradition, and they should perhaps be set down: (1) the problematic character of God and of man's relation to him today, (2) the acceptance of the secular world as normative intellectually and ethically good, (3) the restriction of theological statements to what one can actually affirm oneself, and with this the rejection of certain traditional ideas of tradition and authority, (4) the centrality of Jesus as one who calls us into the world to serve him there, (5) uneasiness with mythological, super-historical, eschatological, supernatural entities or categories. Gilkey goes on to note how each of these five points is a direct attack on a certain portion of the neo-orthodox tradition.)

In a recent critical review of Julian Huxley's *Essays of a Humanist,* Philip Toynbee makes an attack on all psychologically inclined Christians, biologists who listen to Bach, mystical astronomers and humane Catholics. What can we put in their place, he asks.

> And the answer? Simply to wait—on God or whatever it may be, and in the meantime to leave the general alone and to concentrate all our natural energies and curiosities on the specific, the idiosyncratic, the personal.

This combination of waiting and attention on the concrete and personal is the theological point I have been trying to make. Waiting here refers to the whole experience I have called "the death of God," including the attack on religion and the search for a means by which God, not needed, may be enjoyed. We have insisted all along that "death of God" must not be taken as symbolic rhetoric for something else. There really is a sense of not-having, of not-believing, of having lost, not just the idols

or the gods of religion, but God himself. And this is an experience that is not peculiar to a neurotic few, nor is it private or
inward. Death of God is a public event in our history.

Thus we wait, we try out new words, we pray for God to
return, and we seem to be willing to descend into the darkness
of unfaith and doubt that something may emerge on the other
side. In this way, we have tried to interpret and confirm the
mystical images that are so central to the thought of Altizer.[10]

But we do more than play the waiting game. We concen-
trate our energy and passion on the specific, the concrete, the
personal. We turn from the problems of faith to the reality of
love. We walk away from the inner anguish of a Hamlet or an
Oedipus and take up our worldly responsibility with Prospero
and Orestes. As Protestants, we push the movement from church
to world as far as it can go and become frankly worldly men.
And in this world, as we have seen, there is no need for religion
and no need for God. This means that we refuse to consent to
that traditional interpretation of the world as a shadow-screen
of unreality, masking or concealing the eternal which is the
only true reality. This refusal is made inevitable by the scientific revolution of the seventeenth century, and it is this refusal
that stands as a troublesome shadow between ourselves and the
Reformation of the sixteenth. The world of experience is real,
and it is necessary and right to be actively engaged in changing its patterns and structures.

This concentration on the concrete and the worldly says

[10] This emphasis on a passive and letting-be attitude to the world
will suggest several other related themes in current theological thought; for
example, it can be found in a quite different, and most interesting form,
in some of the recent work of Heinrich Ott and of others working with the
problem of the theological use of the later Heidegger. The theme is also
found in the emerging reaction against existentialism in the post-Bultmann-
ians. Ernst Käsemann has written: "The cardinal virtue of the historian
and the beginning of all meaningful hermeneutic is for me the practice of
hearing, which begins simply by letting what is historically foreign maintain its validity and which does not regard rape as the basic form of
engagement." ("Zur Thema der urchristlichen Apokalyptik," *Zeitschrift
für Theologie und Kirche*, LIX, 1962, pp. 262 ff.)

something about the expected context of theology in America today. It means that the theological work that is to be truly helpful—at least for a while—is more likely to come from worldly contexts than ecclesiastical ones, more likely to come from participation in the Negro revolution than from the work of faith and order. But this is no surprise, for ever since the Civil War, ever since the Second Inaugural of Lincoln, the really creative American theological expressions have been worldly rather than ecclesiastical: the work of Walter Rauschenbusch and the work of Reinhold Niebuhr are surely evidence for this. (It is not yet clear how the civil rights movement is going to take on its theological significance, but it has begun, as the radical, southern Negro student comes out of the movement to seminary. He brings a passionate interest in the New Testament doctrines of discipleship and following Jesus and very little interest in the doctrine of sin. One of the most pressing intellectual responsibilities of the Negro student and minister today is that of working out some of the ethical and theological clues that the Negro revolution is teaching him and us all.)

The death of God Protestant, it can be seen, has somewhat inverted the usual relation between faith and love, theology and ethics, God and the neighbor. We are not proceeding from God and faith to neighbor and love, loving in such and such a way because we are loved in such and such a way. We move to our neighbor, to the city and to the world out of a sense of the loss of God. We set aside this sense of loss or death, we note it and allow it to be, neither glad for it, nor insistent that it must be so for all, nor sorry for ourselves. And, for the time of our waiting we place ourselves with our neighbor and enemy in the world.

There is something more than our phrase "waiting for God" that keeps this from sheer atheist humanism. Not only our waiting but our worldly work is Christian too, for our way to our neighbor is not only mapped out by the secular social and psychological and literary disciplines, it is mapped out as well by Jesus Christ and his way to his neighbor. Our ethical existence is partly a time of waiting for God and partly an actual

Christology. Our being in the world, in the city, is not only an obedience to the Reformation formula, from church to world, it is an obedience to Jesus himself. How is this so? How is Jesus being disclosed in the world, being found in the world in our concrete work?

First, Jesus may be concealed in the world, in the neighbor, in this struggle for justice, in that struggle for beauty, clarity, order. Jesus is in the world as masked, and the work of the Christian is to strip off the masks of the world to find him, and, finding him, to stay with him and to do his work. In this sense, the Christian life is not a longing and is not a waiting, it is a going out into the world. The self is discovered, but only incidentally, as one moves out into the world to tear off the masks. Life is a masked ball, a Halloween party, and the Christian life, ethics, love, is that disruptive task of tearing off the masks of the guests to discover the true princess.

In the parable of the last judgment (Matthew 25:34 ff.) the righteous did not know it was Jesus they were serving. The righteous today don't need to know it either, unless they are Christian, in which case they will say that what they are doing is not only service, work, justified for this and that structural reason; it is also an act of unmasking, a looking for, a finding and a staying with Jesus.

In this first sense, the Christian life, ethics, love, is public, outward, visible. It is finding Jesus in your neighbor: "as you did it to one of the least of these my brethren, you did it to me" (Matthew 25:40).

There is another form of the presence of Jesus Christ in the world. Here, we no longer talk about unmasking Jesus who is out there in the world somewhere, we talk about becoming Jesus in and to the world. Here, the Christian life, ethics, love, is first a decision about the self, and then a movement beyond the self into the world.

The form, if not the content, of the parable of the Good Samaritan should be recalled. Jesus is asked a question: which one, among all the many claimants out there, is my neighbor? Jesus answers the question with one of his characteristic non-answers: "Don't look for the neighbor, be one." Or, to put the form of his answer to work on our problem: "Don't look for Jesus out there, in scripture, tradition, sacraments, Ingmar Bergman movies, in the world behind a mask—become Jesus." Become a Christ to your neighbor, as Luther put it.

In this form, the Christian life is not a looking outwards to the world and its claims, it is first a look within in order to become Jesus. "For me to live," cried Paul in one of his most daring utterances, "is Christ." Ethics and love are first a dangerous descent into the self. And in this form, the Christian life, ethics, love, are not so active or worldly. At this point the Christian is the passive man, and doubtless tempted into all of the easily noted dangers of confusing the self with Jesus.

The Christian life as the discernment of Jesus beneath the worldly masks can be called work or interpretation or criticism; while the Christian life as becoming Jesus looks a little different. At this point the Christian is the sucker, the fall guy, the jester, the fool for Christ, the one who stands before Pilate and is silent, the one who stands before power and power-structures and laughs.

Whichever of the paths one takes to find or define Jesus in the world, and perhaps some of us are called to choose both ways, and some only one, the worldliness of the Protestant can never, because of this, have an utterly humanistic form. I may be proposing a too simple marriage between Christology and ethics, a too narrowly ethical approach to Christological problems, but it should at least be noted that however acute the experience of the death of God may be for us, however much silence and loneliness are entailed during our time of waiting for the absent God, we are not particularly cast down or perplexed by this. A form of obedience remains to us in our time of deprivation. We dechristianize no one, we make no virtue of our defects, and we even dare to call men into the worldly arena where men are in need and where Jesus is to be found and served.

W. H.

II
Expositions of the Radical Theology

This article, so much earlier than any of the others in the book, is not included merely because I like it. It is here because the immersion in Dostoevsky that this essay required was the decisive influence in my transition from the neo-orthodox to the radical mode of theological thinking. If I had to allocate the blame for this move, I would doubtless point to Ivan Karamazov and Dietrich Bonhoeffer. In trying to figure out the theological legacy of the Karamazov brothers to us, I sadly realized that we could not go along with Alyosha and that we were all with Ivan.

W. H.

Banished from the Land of Unity

*Dostoevsky's Religious Vision Through the Eyes of
Dmitry, Ivan and Alyosha Karamazov*

"In the presence of God, Dostoevsky remains banished from
the land of unity." (Stefan Zweig, "Dostoevsky" in *Master
Builders.*)

"But it is just in that cold, abominable half despair, half
belief, in that conscious burying oneself alive for grief in the
underworld for forty years, in that acutely recognized and yet
partly doubtful hopelessness of one's position, in that hell of
unsatisfied desires turned inward, in that fever of oscillation,
of resolutions determined for ever and repented of again a
minute later—that the savour of that strange enjoyment of
which I have spoken lies." (Dostoevsky, *Notes from the Underground.*)

The Dostoevsky of *The Brothers Karamazov* has revealed many
faces to the critics. To a Roman Catholic like Romano Guardini,
he is one who describes the disintegration of man when he
departs from the natural tradition of nation and church. To an
Orthodox like Nicholas Berdyaev or V. Ivanov, he is a spokesman for human freedom and a prophet of a new Christianity,
transcending both Roman Catholic and Protestant distortions.
By the Protestant critic he has mainly been valued as the supreme analyst of our cultural despair, particularly that despair
that is inevitable when man turns way from God. A European
intellectual like Hermann Hesse reads the novel as a prediction
of the downfall of Europe: law is at an end, chaos is at hand,

the Karamazov man is taking command.[1] Sigmund Freud, while numbering the man Dostoevsky among the criminals, has called *The Brothers Karamazov* the greatest novel ever written, and the Grand Inquisitor legend one of the artistic pinnacles of the Western world. None of us, apparently, can claim to see Dostoevsky as a whole, so perhaps André Gide was right when he wrote:

> "Dostoevsky remains ever the man of whom there is no way to make use! He is of the stuff which displeases every party."

The task of this essay is to discover what we can about Dostoevsky's own religious vision from a study of *The Brothers Karamazov*. We will take for granted his uncanny insight into our cultural disintegration, adding that this does not exhaust his theological significance. No one can better teach us what our despair is like. But can he teach us how to believe or how to live?

The theme or problem of the novel is the existence of God, though the problem so defined is not identical with the plot. The plot turns on the rivalry between Dmitry and his father for the favors of Grushenka, with the murder of old Karamazov forming the climax. Dmitry is falsely accused, but he accepts his suffering and is changed by it. Smerdyakov, the true murderer and a follower of what he takes to be Ivan's ideas, hangs himself. Ivan partly comes to see that he is the true murderer, collapses under the strain, and may or may not be healed at the end.

The plot begins to fit into the problem as soon as we note that both the literary and theological center of the book lies

---

[1] *Cf.* V. Ivanov, *Freedom and the Tragic Life,* a study of Dostoevsky, Noonday Press, 1957. Nathan Scott's excellent essay, "Dostoevski—Tragedian of the Modern Excursion into Unbelief," chap. 7 in *The Tragic Vision and the Christian Faith,* Association Press, 1958. Nicholas Berdyaev, *Dostoevsky,* Living Age Books, 1957. Also Eduard Thurneysen, *Dostojewski,* Kaiser Verlag, München, 1930 (E. T. John Knox Press, 1906), an extreme and verbose but illuminating study of Dostoevsky as a forerunner of the theology of crises. *In Sight of Chaos,* translated by S. Hudson, Verlag Seldwyla, Zurich, 1923, p. 14.

in the character of the three (legitimate) Karamazov sons, Ivan, Dmitry, Alyosha, and their relationship to the death of their father. The three brothers, taken together, are a portrait both of Russian man and of Dostoevsky himself: what he knew he was and what he hoped to become. He *is*, indeed, *The Brothers Karamazov*.

This can be established by noting the setting of the novel in Dostoevsky's own life. On May 16, 1878, he lost his two-year-old son, Alexey, after an epileptic attack. Later, the hero of the novel was to bear the boy's name. Dostoevsky was in despair and hungered for religious consolation. His wife urged him to visit a famous monastery, and late in June he did so, accompanied by Vladimir Solovyev, who may have been a source for both the character and the ideas of Alyosha. He went in search of faith, but the evidence is that he did not receive the consolation he expected. There was no one in the real monastery faintly resembling the saintly Zossima.

But the journey that really set the novel in motion seems to have been one taken the year before, in June 1877, when he visited some property once owned by his father. This return to a familiar place of his past brought not only his childhood but his whole life before him. Here it was that his father had been murdered; here it was that Dostoevsky himself had probably raped a young girl, many years before. It is not arbitrary, therefore, to see the novel that grew from these two journeys as in part an attempt at self-analysis.

If it is, we can understand why there is so much about the special character of the Karamazovs as a family. The family as a whole is marked by unique traits: shame and self-pity (p. 46),[2] sensuality (pp. 89, 90, 824), unbeliefs. Even Alyosha confesses several times that he too is a Karamazov (pp. 254, 257) and once that he does not believe in God (p. 257).

The similarities between the brothers must be carefully observed before we can trust ourselves to note the obvious

[2] Page references in the text of the essay refer to the Penguin Classics edition of the novel translated by David Magarshack.

differences. All the brothers, in one way or another, desire the death of their father: "who does not desire the death of his father," Ivan had once cried out. And each of the brothers is partly guilty of his father's death: Ivan most of all because he did not prevent the murder which he knew was to happen, and because his own "creation" Smerdyakov actually did the deed; Dmitry, because he wished for his father's death; Alyosha, because he was falsely detached from the world and did not use the new courage derived from his conversion to prevent the disaster.

Dmitry is perhaps the truest *external* portrait of Dostoevsky: noble but uncontrolled, rake and trouble-maker. This is the Dostoevsky who was the compulsive gambler, complaining of his poverty. Dmitry's love of the prostitute Grushenka reminds us of Dostoevsky's own attraction to Suslova. But Dmitry was the son of old Karamazov's first wife; Ivan and Alyosha were sons of the second. We may conclude that if Dmitry is more *externally* related to Dostoevsky, the real *inner* tension in Dostoevsky is that symbolized by Ivan and Alyosha. The novel as a study in Dostoevsky's struggle with God has its focus in the tension between Ivan and Alyosha.

But this is not just a tension between Alyosha as believer and Ivan as unbeliever. Each of the brothers is himself a divided man. There is a kind of God in Ivan's heart, for Ivan cannot be described as an unbeliever at all. He accepts God but rejects his world. There is a God in Dmitry's heart for all his confusion (pp. 141, 430, 485, 694-95, 700-01, 822); and there is unbelief in gentle Alyosha (pp. 88-90, 125). Each of the brothers represents the sensuality of the Karamazovs looking for the new man to be born. "I'm the same as you," Alyosha once said to Dmitry. "The steps are the same—I'm on the lowest one, and you're above, somewhere on the thirteenth. It's one and the same thing" (p. 125).

Each of the brothers, then (we are not including the "brother" who was the actual murderer) participates in the death of the father. Does the death of the father here stand for the death of the Father, the death of God? Can we then say that Dostoevsky identifies the plot (the story of the murder) with the theme (the problem of God) by having both speak of the death of the Father? All the brothers, therefore, participate in the death of God. How can one return to the Father when he is dead? This is Dostoevsky's real religious problem in this novel. It is not the actual emptiness of man's life but the possible emptiness of the heavens that really terrifies Dostoevsky.

Dmitry once said to Alyosha: "Don't think that I'm just a boor of an officer who does nothing but drink brandy and leads a life of lust and depravity . . . I scarcely think of anything but of this degraded man" (p. 122). Of concrete suffering man, he means. Dmitry is of course a sensualist, without discipline or restraint. But like many sensualists he has a genuine sensitivity, especially to the suffering of the innocent. He is rough and uneducated, but he has a highly developed sense of pity and honor. He is coarse and crude, full of compassion and longing. His dream-vision of the starving child will never leave him; his joyful willingness to accept his conviction, even though he is innocent of the crime, attests to a real "conversion." He will wipe away the sufferings of Russia by suffering himself for a crime he did not commit (p. 898). He rejects, at the end, both suicide and cynicism, and even in the mines to which he is to be sent, he sees that God will be present. "If they banish God from the earth," he cries, "we shall need him under the earth! . . . And then shall we, the men beneath the ground, sing from the bowels of the earth our tragic hymn to God, in whom there is gladness!" (pp. 694-5). This earth knows neither God nor human brotherhood; but both God and brotherhood will be affirmed from the underground. In this way Zossima's vision of a united humanity will be achieved, and we can understand why, early in the novel, the elder so mysteriously bowed before the troubled Dmitry.

This is a fascinating and moving eschatological vision, but it is not Christian. The basis for the new unity between man and God in suffering is an identification with Mother Earth. Dmitry is Demeter, the earth-god, and his religious vision is a pagan one. Notice the fragment from Schiller that is to be the song of the new underground man:

> That from the worst unto the better
> Man his soul may raise up high,
> He must join his ancient mother,
> Mother earth his best ally.
>   (p. 122; the lines are from
>   "Eleusinian Festival")

Thus Dmitry's Karamazov-sensuality is transformed into a new and more spiritual form. But even in his conversion he is still a Karamazov. Yet, this is a real conversion. The final note is one of hope, and Zossima's words find real fruition in him. But it is a conversion to the universal humanism and optimism of Schiller. It is a conversion to the earth, and perhaps to a mystical vision of a united nation, but not to the Christian God.

The faith of Ivan and Alyosha is a more complicated problem. We will have occasion later to be reminded of Dmitry's vision, for Alyosha's "conversion" will prove to be essentially the same. And we will conclude that Dostoevsky did in fact believe that he had broken through his own unbelief. He did think that he had gone beyond the death of God. He found what he called God and Christ. But what he found was a God who behaved very much like a Karamazov; and his Christ was the vague figure of Ivan's distorted Grand Inquisitor legend.

Ivan, we are told again and again by commentators, is a figure of atheism and unbelief. His life and ideas are signs of what happens when the death of God is taken seriously. Autam Yarmolinsky reminds us of the sense in which Ivan may be seen as Dostoevsky himself.

> There can be small doubt as to the identification of the novelist with Ivan Karamazov. . . . Ivan has Dostoevsky's lust for life, his acute sense of evil, his capacity for cruelty to others—particularly those he loved—and toward himself, and that duality Dostoevsky recognized to be his own, a source of perpetual strength and perverse pleasure. Was it true that when he had Ivan say that he could not understand how it was possible for a man to love his neighbor, he was describing precisely his own sentiments?

To Berdyaev it is obvious why Ivan cannot love his neighbor: he has rejected God's existence. It is impossible to love man apart from God, Berdyaev asserts. "Outside of the Christian conception, love is an illusion and a lie." This conclusion seems both silly and false, but apart from that, Berdyaev's whole point is based on a faulty reading of the evidence. Ivan is not unable to love his neighbor, and Ivan is not a simple atheist or unbeliever. Doubtless Dostoevsky did put much of himself into Ivan, but not into an unbelieving Ivan. He put himself rather into an Ivan with an overwhelming compassion and love for the world, and into an Ivan who "accepted" God.

There are two ways of reading the struggle of Ivan: one *existential* or *personal*, the other *theological*. The literary critics usually stress the first, and it is partly correct. Ivan has the Karamazov vitality and lust for life, and he is also the man of reason bent on understanding the life he is living. He says,

> I've asked myself many times: is there in the world any despair that would overcome this frenzied and, perhaps, indecent thirst for life in me, and I've come to the conclusion that, perhaps, there isn't. . . . However much I may disbelieve in the order of things, I still love the sticky little leaves that open up in the spring, I love the blue sky. . . . It's not a matter of intellect or logic. You love it all with your inside, with your belly (pp. 268-69).

The warmth of his love and the coldness of his mind give Ivan two different answers to the problem of the freedom of the will. His mind affirms that man is free. His "poem" about the Grand Inquisitor tells us this; and this freedom is what finally leads him to rebel against God. But Ivan's actions convince him that there is no freedom, that all men are fated to be parricides, that no one can escape the curse. So man's denial of God is not a free choice, it is a mysterious and fateful necessity.

We can see this tension as we trace Ivan's actions just after the murder of his father. He had actually contemplated murder, but then he had suddenly left for Moscow. When he hears of the murder he returns home, learns who the murderer really was, and becomes more and more oppressed by his own guilt in the months before the trial. He realizes finally that he did in fact murder his father, thus confirming Zossima's words about our responsibility for all men. This insight is a victory for his conception of freedom, and he resolves to make a full confession at the trial. Just before the trial, he has his dream-vision of the Devil and falls into his old confusion. Ivan falls asleep after the interview with the Devil, and Alyosha remarks that he will wake with either the light of truth or the light of hate in his heart. At the trial, however, his testimony is neither truthful nor hateful; it is confused, for he is already seriously ill with brain-fever. Ivan's testimony convinces no one, and it leaves Dmitry worse off than before. Ivan tried to acknowledge his responsibility for the crime, but was either unwilling or unable to pay the price for his involvement in suffering and humility.

Is Ivan's future one of salvation and hope, as Dmitry's apparently is? We must say yes, even though we know nothing of Ivan beyond his mental illness. But Alyosha had pointed out that Ivan's illness was not merely confusion, but a partial sign of hope. Alyosha remarked that Ivan's decision to confess and to try to help his unjustly accused brother was a decision for virtue by a man who did not believe in virtue. In Alyosha's words, we can detect the possibility of as real a hope for Ivan as there is for Dmitry: "he has served something he does not believe in." God, in whom Ivan did not naturally believe, gained a hold over his heart; and yet, Alyosha remarks, his heart still refused to give in (p. 771).[3]

So Ivan's struggle is more than a conventional one between logic and life, between emancipated intellectualism and the unshakeable Karamazov lust. It is mainly a struggle about God.

[3] And, as Thurneysen says, "even when one is in hell, one can be forgiven," op. cit., p. 61. Zossima speaks a word, earlier in the novel, that may help us understand Dostoevky's attitude to Ivan: "those who are apart from Christianity and in revolt against it are none the less still personifications of Christ in their essence, and such they will remain." Thus Ivan not merely will be, but already is, in Christ.

Is God dead? This is the real question that drives Ivan mad, for he cannot give a simple "yes" to it. The same question drove Nietzsche mad, and it may have very nearly driven Dostoevsky mad as well.

The struggle is not a simple one. It is set in motion by the problem of suffering and by Ivan's confessed inability to see anything more than three dimensions to life. He refuses to affirm an over-all harmony merely to explain suffering. His terrible confession to Alyosha in the tavern is no simple atheistic indictment of religion. It is such a terrible and true picture that it has the power to threaten our most secure religious foundations.

> "Well, this may surprise you, but perhaps I accept God," Ivan laughed (p. 273). "I accept God plainly and simply. But there's this that has to be said: if God really exists and if he really has created the world, then, as we all know, he created it in accordance with the Euclidean geometry.... I have a Euclidean, an earthly mind, and so how can I be exected to solve problems which are not of this world?" (p. 274). And so I accept God, and I accept him not only without reluctance, but what's more, I accept his divine wisdom and purpose—which are completely beyond our comprehension. I believe in the underlying order and meaning of life.... Anyway, you'd be surprised to learn, I think, that in the final result I refuse to accept this world of God's, and though I know that it exists, I absolutely refuse to admit its existence. Please understand, it is not God that I do not accept, but the world he has created" (p. 275).

Ivan continues, and makes the same point in a different way. The sufferings of humanity in general are too vast a subject to tackle. "Perhaps," he says,

> "we'd better confine ourselves to the sufferings of children" (p. 277). "No innocent must suffer for another, and such innocents, too! You may be surprised at me, Alyosha, for I too love little children terribly" (p. 278). "Oh, all that my pitiful earthly Euclidean mind can grasp is that suffering exists, that no one is to blame, that effect follows cause, simply and directly, that everything flows and finds its level—but then this is only Eu-

clidean nonsense. I know that and I refuse to live by it" (p. 285). "Listen: if all have to suffer so as to buy eternal harmony by their suffering, what have the children to do with it—tell me, please? . . . I understand solidarity in sin among men, I understand solidarity in retribution, too, but, surely, there can be no solidarity in sin with children, and if it is really true that they share their fathers' responsibility for all their fathers' crimes, then that truth is not, of course, of this world, and it's incomprehensible to me" (p. 286). "I want to forgive. I want to embrace. I don't want any more suffering. And if the sufferings of children go to make up the sum of sufferings which is necessary for the purchase of truth, then I say beforehand that the entire truth is not worth such a price. . . . I don't want harmony. I don't want it, out of the love I bear to mankind. . . . I'd rather remain with my suffering unavenged and my indignation unappeased, *even if I were wrong*. Besides, too high a price has been placed on harmony. We cannot afford to pay so much for admission. . . . It is not God that I do not accept, Alyosha, I merely most respectfully return him the ticket" (p. 287).

Alyosha can only reply, softly, "this is rebellion." And of course it is. But it is a rebellion that has a strange and poignant love at the center of it. Albert Camus, in *The Rebel,* had this insight which makes his interpretation of Ivan much clearer than many of our Christian ones.

Then we understand that rebellion cannot exist without a strange form of love. Those who find no rest in God or in history are condemned to live for those who, like themselves, cannot live: in fact, for the humiliated. The most pure form of the movement of rebellion is thus crowned with the heart-rending cry of Karamazov: if all are not saved, what good is the salvation of one only?

In this conversation between Ivan and Alyosha, we are in quite a different world from that suggested by Ivan's hypothesis as it is reported in the novel from time to time: "if God does not exist, then everything is permitted." Much of the critical discussion about Ivan's religious views assumes that this declaration is at the center of his thought. But this hypothetical statement is interesting because Dostoevsky never has Ivan make it directly. It is mentioned several times, but only by someone else who has heard Ivan state it. Miusov and Rakitin report it; Smerdyakov suggests that he has also learned it from Ivan. In the dream-vision (p. 763), the Devil speaks of the man-god who will make his appearance after the idea of God is destroyed, but this has the effect of suggesting that Ivan rejects the idea. For though Ivan saw that the Devil was a part of himself, he was only the vulgar and stupid part. Ivan never seriously or directly affirms this idea himself. Indeed, only once does he ever directly declare his disbelief in God, and that is in the somewhat playful discussion over brandy with his father.

In Ivan's confession to Alyosha, God is not dead, he is "accepted." "Everything is permitted if God does not exist," then, seems rather to be a mask that Ivan hides behind. It is a statement he enjoys making at parties, but his serious problem is not the non-existence of God at all. As a matter of fact, the existence of God gives Ivan far more agony than his non-existence ever could. This is not unbelief or atheism, it is a testing of God on the basis of a standard of justice. And God fails the test. If God exists, he cries out, I will still reject his world, for it is unjust that so much pain and suffering should be necessary. What Ivan really rejects, Camus points out, is

> the profound relationship, introduced by Christianity, between suffering and truth. Ivan's most profound utterance, the one which opens the deepest chasms beneath the rebel's feet, is his *even if:* "I would persist in my indignation, even if I were wrong."

Indeed, the burden of the passage is just that: God does exist, but Ivan returns to him the ticket of admission, he rejects his world. In one sense, Ivan's rebellion is a true one, since he protests in the name of something. He is no nihilist. He protests in the name of the suffering of children. In another sense, Ivan does not have the power to carry this authentic rebellion out; for when it comes to the test at the trial, he cannot make himself comprehensible. His inability at the trial to admit his involvement in the death of his father, to carry out the logic of his true rebellion, is caused by the very mental anguish the true rebellion itself has brought on. Thus Camus' description of Ivan's rebellion as nihilistic and false is only partly true. In principle, Ivan does rebel against God on behalf of the suffering of children. He thus meets Camus' test of a true rebel as one who knows what he rebels on behalf of as well as what he rebels against.

Dostoevsky, through Ivan, faced a problem that modern Christian thought has tended to avoid: the suffering of children. So he (Ivan, and Dostoevsky too?) accepts God and refuses to believe in him or his world. Ivan persists in his rebellion, and is driven partly mad by it. Is this an inevitable fate for those who cannot break through their rebellion? If God had not spoken out of the whirlwind, would not Job himself have gone mad?

Ivan's struggle was not merely one between two psychological dispositions: logic and thirst for life. It was a theological struggle. It was not that he decided to deny God and choose man and his freedom,[4] but that he wanted to be a theologian without a theodicy. Karl Barth's *Romans* is a similar attempt. Ivan's partly failed and partly succeeded. It failed in that he was driven into what Dostoevsky calls "brain-fever," and thus became unable to save Dmitry at the trial. But it succeeded too, for it led him, at least for a moment, to accept responsibility for his father's death. Ivan is a man in whom belief and rebellion are fatefully conjoined. In the interview with the Devil, Ivan says: "you're the embodiment of myself, but only of one side of me" (p. 749). A moment later, he cries out: "you're stupid and vulgar" (p. 750). To be able to say this is not to be wholly

---

[4] This is how Berdyaev reads Ivan, and he is prompted to describe Ivan's brain-fever as the necessary result of choosing freedom without God. The divided self portrayed in the interview with the Devil is what, according to Berdyaev, comes to all men who try to choose man and his freedom without choosing God. But Ivan does not reject God, he "chooses" him, he accepts him.

mad or wholly unbelieving. Rebellion and belief stand together in Ivan as in his creator. Ivan asks the Devil if God exists. The Devil replies: "My dear fellow, I really don't know" (p. 755). Ivan replies, you don't know, even though you see him? And then, with a kind of triumph: "You are *I*, you *are* I and nothing more! You are rubbish. You are my fancy!" (p. 756). A few pages later there are some words of the Devil, whom Ivan has identified with himself, that may be as clear an insight into Ivan's actual faith as we have.

> I keep you dangling between belief and disbelief by turns, and I don't mind admitting that I have a reason for it. It's the new method, sir. For when you lose your faith in me completely, you will at once begin assuring me to my face that I'm not a dream, but do really exist. (p. 759)

To examine Ivan's poem about the Grand Inquisitor is to find the same mixture of perversion and insight, rebellion and belief.[5] The legend of the Grand Inquisitor is often taken as the spiritual center of the novel. It may be, but it is also the most difficult part of the novel to get clear. Whose side is Ivan

[5] Dostoevsky has a special meaning for the word *atheist* that does perhaps fit Ivan. In a fragment from *The Possessed* that did not appear in the final draft, but which has been published recently under the title *Stavrogin's Confession,* the monk Tikhon says: "Complete atheism is more respectable than worldly indifference. . . . A complete atheist stands on the last rung but one before absolute faith (he may or may not step higher), but an indifferent man has no longer any faith at all, nothing but an ugly fear, and that only on rare occasions, if he is a sentimental man." This is acute, and it also looks like a piece of both self-description and self-defense on Dostoevsky's part. An atheist in Zossima's and Tikhon's sense, then, Ivan perhaps is; and Dostoevsky as well: passionately concerned, a step away from absolute faith, never confident about getting there, usually sure he never will. Thurneysen distinguishes between the true and the demonic atheist in Ivan: the first sees through the dishonesty of most theodicies and sees the godlessness of most religion; the second exalts man into the place of God. (*Op. cit.,* p. 53.) If this is the kind of atheism Dostoevsky finds in himself, we can understand Père De Lubac's remark that "anyone whose chief desire is for reassurance will not take Dostoevsky as his confidant." See H. De Lubac, *The Drama of Atheist Humanism,* part III, "Dostoevsky as Prophet," Sheed and Ward, London, 1949, p. 179.

on? Whose side is Dostoevsky on? What is the relation of Ivan's Christ to the Christ of the Christian faith? Does Ivan take this "stupid poem of a stupid student," as he calls it, seriously? Are we meant to? Or should we conclude that this is a piece of imaginative literature and therefore be content to allow it to remain in the limbo of ambiguous works that illuminate and excite without being understood?

Commentators all have their axes to grind. Roman Catholics (like Guardini) assure us that we need not take Dostoevsky's anti-Roman bias seriously, and that we must interpret him by laws he was not fully conscious of. We are often told by others that the legend is a prophetic warning against political totalitarianisms. Berdyaev tells us that this portrait of Christ as absolute freedom is authentically Christian and our absolute model. For Eduard Thurneysen the legend is an analysis of how man can expect no earthly or spiritual security in this life. He has only the promise that God will be present to him in his insecurity. Of course, he says, the burden of freedom is too great for man. Of course man must reject that God who can be too easily grasped by miracle. Of course man wants "to believe in a God that is familiar, comprehensible, and testable." The true God is beyond all human need and ability, and thus Dostoevsky is portrayed as a forerunner of Barth.

So, reeling from all this good advice, we reread the legend; our love for the Christ moves into dissatisfaction and bewilderment. Our rejection of the Inquisitor becomes modified and nearly transformed into affection as we discover that his analysis of man's fear of freedom is in line with that of the latest psychologists and sociologists, and that his doctrine of man partakes of today's fashionable pessimism.

I claim that the message of the legend is deeply unclear and finally impossible to discover because Ivan did not know himself clearly, and because Dostoevsky did not either. Perhaps the legend was written to gain clarity, but the mixture of rebellion and belief that wrote it is the very mixture that comes out of it as we read it today. We rebel at and believe the cardinal; we rebel at and believe this Christ.

D. H. Lawrence in an interesting essay "The Grand Inquisitor by F. M. Dostoevsky" appearing in a collection of his papers, *Phoenix*, describes Middleton Murry remarking to him that the whole clue to Dostoevsky is in the Grand Inquisitor story. Lawrence tells us he replied: "Why? It seems to me just rubbish." He goes on to say that the whole passage seems to him just a cynical pose, a piece of showing off. He adds that it is also a final and unanswerable indictment of Christ, "a deadly, devastating summing-up, unanswerable because borne out by the long experience of humanity. It is reality versus illusion, and the illusion was Jesus', while time itself retorts with the reality."

The illusion of Jesus was his estimate of man, Lawrence claims. It is not diabolical to deny human perfectibility, he notes. The church has always denied it, at least until the Enlightenment. Man has always needed mystery, miracle and authority, and always will. It is not weakness to need these; Jesus himself offered them:

> And if Jesus cast aside miracle in the Temptation, still there is miracle again in the Gospels. And if Jesus refused the earthly bread, still he said: "In my Father's house are many mansions." And for authority: "Why call ye me Lord, Lord, and do not the things which I say?" (p. 288)

Lawrence does not see, by noting that Jesus in the gospels does not withhold miracle, mystery and authority, that he has questioned the validity of Dostoevsky's picture of Jesus. He continues to claim that Dostoevsky has demonstrated the irrelevance of Jesus as he really is. Most men, Lawrence claims,

> *cannot* choose between good and evil, because it is so extremely difficult to know which is which, especially in crucial cases: and . . . *cannot* see the difference between life-values and money-values: they can only see money-values; even nice simple people who *live* by the life-values, kind and natural, yet can only estimate value in terms of money. (p. 290)

Jesus finally fails, Lawrence goes on, because his demand of freedom is too difficult for man. Christianity is the true ideal, but it is impossible because it puts greater burdens on man than he is able to bear. The Grand Inquisitor has discovered that men must be loved more tolerantly than Jesus loved them, for what is, not for what ought to be. Jesus loved mankind, Lawrence says—following Dostoevsky carefully—for what it ought to be, free and limitless. The Inquisitor loved it for what it is, with all its limitations. And the Inquisitor, rightly for Lawrence, contends that his is the kinder love.

There is a good case to be made for Lawrence's objection to Dostoevsky's Jesus. There may well be an element of forgiveness in the Inquisitor's relation to his flock that we do not find in the attitude of Dostoevsky's Jesus. But of course, Lawrence may only have proved the irrelevance of Dostoevsky's Jesus, and not the biblical one.

Lawrence makes a final comment that alters his whole interpretation of Christ in the legend. Up to the end of his essay, Christ is rejected because he was too pure, too irrelevant to the reality of human sin, too optimistic. But, Lawrence concludes, this Christ is converted at the end by the Inquisitor's words, and his kiss of the old man is a kiss of acquiescence. Here Christ submits to the cardinal; he admits that his view of love is profounder than his own. The guilty savior asks to be forgiven.

> Jesus kisses the Inquisitor: Thank you, you are right, wise, old man! Alyosha kisses Ivan: Thank you, brother, you are right, you take a burden off me! So why should Dostoevsky drag in Inquisitors and *autos-da-fe,* and Ivan wind up so morbidly suicidal. Let them be glad they've found the truth again. (pp. 290-91)

This is certainly a possible interpretation of the kiss. Zossima taught Alyosha to kiss the earth, to become one with it, and this was an act of identification. Dmitry had sung a song about man's union with Mother Earth. Alyosha, in the "conversion" scene after the death of Zossima, kisses the earth in an act that Dostoevsky intends to have decisive meaning for the youngest brother. So there is some evidence that the kiss might be an act of acquiescence.

Usually it is interpreted as a kiss of forgiveness from Christ to the saintly sinner. As Thurneysen puts this conventional view, "this is the answer which Dostoevsky . . . wants to give to man in his tremendous godlessness."

But it is more likely that something between forgiveness and acquiescence will come closest to the truth. Does not the use of the kiss in the rest of the novel suggest that Ivan means to say here that Christ admits his own involvement in the sin of the cardinal? There is ambiguity in the character of this Christ; even in him there is that old mixture of the highest and the lowest that so fascinated Dostoevsky. This is a kiss of understanding. The cardinal is man at the highest stage of historical development: unselfish, honest, wanting nothing for himself. Perhaps in this kiss we can hear the silent Christ saying something like this: "I nearly became what you are, and even so, I have made many men into what you now are. I am guilty for what you have become." If this is right, then in this kiss which is both demonic and compassionate, Christ fulfills the vision of Zossima, of which the three brothers, even at the end, possess only fragments.

Lawrence strikes wildly in many directions in his interpretation, and scores a few direct blows, but is finally either unable or unwilling to distinguish between Dostoevsky's silent weakling and the Christ of the New Testament. Even so, he is right when he says:

> As always in Dostoevsky, the amazing perspicacity is mixed with ugly perversity. Nothing is pure. His wild love for Jesus is mixed with perverse and poisonous hate of Jesus: his moral hostility to the devil is mixed with secret worship of the devil. Dostoevsky is always perverse, always impure, always an evil thinker and a marvellous seer. (p. 285)

Another original (and perverse) interpretation of the legend is that of the Roman Catholic Guardini. A Protestant is almost obliged to call part of Guardini's interpretation perverse. Guardini denies that the legend is really speaking against authoritarian religion. Of course, Dostoevsky hated Romanism, he grants, but Guardini also grants to himself the right to interpret Dostoevsky as not really being against Rome, "in spite of himself," because he is able to see deeper levels in Dostoevsky of which he was unaware. But this is not a serious flaw. Dostoevsky has a way of tempting us to see only what we want to see, even when we look very carefully and try to see everything.

Guardini says much that is trenchant and true. The legend, he tells us, must be seen as Ivan's elaborate justification for his own views. Since the Christ of the legend is so patently inadequate to the world, Ivan is saying, what can man do but try to find his own way? "This Christ makes Ivan right," Guardini says.[6] It is clear that Ivan has much in common with the Inquisitor. Ivan, like the old man, "rejects the world and wishes to tear it from the hands of God, since he made it badly, with the pretension of organizing it differently and in a superior manner than its original author."[7] Or again, and more clearly:

> This false Christ makes the transformation of the real world by a true Christianity impossible and so delivers it as a prey to usurpation—to the usurpation of Ivan. (p. 67)

Guardini assumes that Ivan believed himself to be describing the Christ that the Christian affirms and the careful non-Christian rejects. Alyosha, after all, at the close of the legend, declares to Ivan that the poem is "in praise of Jesus and not in his disparagement as—as you wanted it to be" (p. 305). In my view, Ivan had not really made up his mind whether he

---

[6] Romano Guardini, "The Legend of the Grand Inquisitor," *Cross Currents*, vol. iii, no. 1, Fall, 1952, p. 66. It should be noted that Guardini assumes, more decisively than I do, that "if God does not exist, everything is permitted" is a fundamental part of Ivan's intellectual equipment.

[7] *Ibid.* Thurneysen reads the whole Grand Inquisitor legend as a modern temptation of Christ by the Devil. The cardinal is the Devil; the cardinal is also Ivan; and finally, as the dream-vision proves, Ivan himself becomes the Devil, "for what is the Devil but the spirit who knows the true eternal God—not just the man-god—and who still rejects Him." *Op. cit.*, p. 57. But this kind of precise identification is not what we find in the novel itself. See pp. 306, 308 of text.

himself intended praise or disparagement. But both brothers agree that the poem does in fact describe Jesus Christ.[8]

It is right to insist that this is not the Christian picture of Christ. D. H. Lawrence has already pointed out that the rejector of miracles still performed them, the rejector of authority claimed it from man, and, we might add, the rejector of mystery came proclaiming the mystery of the kingdom of God. The frail silence of Dostoevsky's figure does not really convince us. This is a Christ who has come from nowhere and who returns nowhere. There is no God beyond him, there is no forgiveness or redemption through him. Dostoevsky's Christ is an ikon, an ascetic who has lost touch with the real world of ordinary men. This is how Guardini makes his case:

> This Christ does not have that holy relationship of love for the real world which purifies it and renews it; he is simply compassion, bearing an invitation to leave the world. This Christ is detached; we might even dare to say that he is an egotist. . . . His figure leaves an impression on us, but it is purely imaginary and leads to nothing. The disturbance that he brings gives rise to confusion and finally results in despair.[9]

Berdyaev, on the other hand, believes Dostoevsky's Christ to be simply absolute freedom. He is silent because the principle of freedom cannot be expressed in words without some form of authority being suggested. Historic Christianity has never actualized this radical freedom, and therefore historic Christianity must be judged by Dostoevsky's Christ. But it is clear to Berdyaev that the gospels support his identification of Christ and freedom.

> Therein lies the radical secret of Jesus Christ, the secret of freedom. It needed an extraordinary freedom of spirit, a prodigy of

[8] De Lubac agrees with Alyosha, and remarks (in direct contrast to Guardini) that the poem is really a hymn of praise to Jesus: Is this the deliberate effect of consummate art? May it not, rather, be the spontaneous result of a love which, even when it has to let the adversary speak, cannot wholly restrain itself? In any case, Dostoevsky here reveals the depth of his heart. *Op. cit.*, p. 185.

[9] *Op. cit.*, p. 64.

free faith . . . to see God beneath the appearance of a bondsman, and when Simon Peter said to Jesus, "Thou art the Christ, the Son of the living God," he made an act of freedom.[10]

But Peter's confession is surely not adequately described as an act of freedom. In Matthew 16:17 Jesus states that it is not Peter's freedom, not "flesh and blood," but "my Father who is in heaven" that made Peter's words possible. Peter's confession was not so much an act of freedom as an act of faith in response to the grace of God. Freedom is involved, and something more. Berdyaev has apparently chosen to stand with Dostoevsky's Christ against both scripture and historic Christianity.

Dostoevsky's Christ *is* the idea of freedom, and it clears the air to be able to see this. But for us this is precisely the reason why this Christ cannot be identified with Jesus Christ of the New Testament record.

In his discussion of the relation of the ultimate to the penultimate, Dietrich Bonhoeffer points to two false ethical solutions which he calls compromise and radicalism. Compromise sees what needs to be done, and in order to do it, accepts the world in all its brutality. The Grand Inquisitor stands here. Radicalism sees only the goal, and every other consideration is rejected. Dostoevsky's Christ is here. Neither way is possible, though Dostoevsky showed us only the two: the anarchy of love, or the ruling elect giving man what he wishes. Today we know too much to be satisfied with this simple set of alternatives, but too little to coherently state a third way. The love of Christ, freely accepted by man, does make us truly free. But we also know something else. Men may do without spiritual bread; they may even do without love; but they cannot do without earthly bread.

I have been shouting "unclear" at both Dmitry and Ivan up to now, and consequently at Dostoevsky's religious vision. Perhaps this is the shout of an earthly Euclidean mind; perhaps it is the shout of a moralist or theologian too coarse-grained

[10] *Op. cit.*, p. 79. Cf. pp. 189, 204.

to discern the limpid clarity behind the warring images. To me "unclear" means two intelligible things. Dostoevsky's religious vision is internally unclear, unclear on its own terms. Dostoevsky does not know the way he wishes to go. Is the way Dmitry's sensual humility—singing praises of the earth-god from the subterranean depths, or worse (if he and Grushenka made good their escape to America), from some farm in up-state New York? Or is the way of Ivan and his theological rebellion one of holding to God for fear of annihilation, but hating him and his world, and with equal passion asserting the reality of a human freedom that he denies by his quixotic behavior at the time of the trial? Unclarity in this first sense lies in the material. Then, the God of Ivan in the tavern-scene is unclear;[11] the God-less Christ of the legend is unclear; the earth-god of Dmitry is unclear. None of them can be related to distinctive Christian affirmations.

Many would agree that Dostoevsky was tempted to go Ivan's way and made Ivan's position as persuasive to himself as he could. But it didn't work, and in the course of the novel he rejects Ivan and gives himself to Alyosha. The youngest brother is Dostoevsky's sole claim to be taken seriously as a religious guide.

This view may be correct, and certainly Alyosha is to be taken seriously as a religious guide, whatever that means. But is there anything essentially new about Alyosha's religious vision? Or is it, too, "unclear"?

Alyosha is not a successful character from a literary point of view. In the first half of the novel, he apparently interested Dostoevsky. But at the time of the trial, he passes into the shadows, only to emerge rather awkwardly at the end. There is no convincing relationship established between Alyo-

[11] There are really two images of God in Ivan's discussion with Alyosha. One is the God who explains suffering by positing an over-all unity to things; the other is the Tormentor who compels Ivan to refuse to trust in the first. The first image is dead for Ivan (and for us). The second, Ivan's—and perhaps Dostoevsky's—true God, is not dead for us for it is very similar to the God of modern theology.

sha's virtue and the world in which he moves. In one sense he has a kind of virtue or innocence. But he is also a Karamazov.

> What we have here is "the earth-bound Karamazov force," as Father Paissy expressed it the other day, earth-bound, unrestrained and crude. I don't even know whether the spirit of God moves over that force. All I know is that I, too, am a Karamazov. I a monk, a monk? Am I a monk, Lise? I believe you said I was a monk a moment ago.
> Yes, I did.
> And yet I don't think I even believe in God.
> You don't believe? What's the matter with you? Lise said softly and guardedly.
> But Alyosha made no answer. There was something very mysterious and very subjective in these sudden words of his, something that he perhaps did not understand himself, but that undoubtedly worried him. (p. 257)

At this time of the crisis in Alyosha's life, when he was trying to face the fact of the decomposition of Zossima's corpse, Dostoevsky tells us both that Alyosha's faith was strong and that it was unsophisticated and inadequately trained (pp. 396-97). Indeed, at this time (p. 400), Alyosha even blurted out for himself the words he had recently heard his brother say: "I haven't taken up arms against God. . . . I simply 'don't accept his world.'" Again, Dostoevsky seems almost to take delight in showing that at this very time when he was filled with a universal love for all men, Alyosha nevertheless forgot to visit Dmitry who needed him, and forgot to take the money to Ilyusha's father as he had promised to do (pp. 397-98).

Just before his death, Zossima had been speaking to Alyosha, and part of his teaching at that time is a clue to what is to follow. "Fall upon the earth," Zossima had said,

> when left alone, and kiss it, drench it with your tears, and the earth will bring forth fruit from your tears even if no one has heard or seen you in your loneliness. . . . Kiss the earth ceaselessly and love it insatiably. Love all men, love everything, seek that rapture and ecstasy. Water the earth with the tears of your joy and love those tears. (pp. 378-79)

When Zossima died, it was generally expected that his body, like the bodies of traditional holy men of the past, would be exempt from corruption. Alyosha expected this miracle to take place as a matter of course. Just before he died, Zossima had read to Alyosha the words of John 12:24, and had solemnly urged him to remember them.

Alyosha returns to the elder's cell after his death and hears Father Paissy reading the story of the miracle at Cana. Everything seems ready for the miracle of incorruption to take place. But it does not. Dostoevsky himself describes what happens rather gently: "What happened was that an odour of corruption began to come from the coffin" (p. 387). Rakitin puts it more bluntly: "his elder is stinking the place up."

Dostoevsky does not consider the corruption of the body a repulsive thing. It is the ultimate reality, and this event alone is able to penetrate Alyosha's innocence. All mortal men, even holy men, do in fact return to the earth. Alyosha does not yet see why his innocence had to be shattered. He seeks out Grushenka, hoping, he says, to find a "wicked soul"; but he finds instead a "loving heart" that lifts him out of his depths. He returns to the cell and prays.

Dostoevsky is preparing us for a miracle of grace, but he suggests that a true miracle is not one that transforms the remains of a saint who has done his work, but one which touches a young man about to enter the world. Alyosha had assumed that the elder's final words meant that he, Zossima, would rise again from the earth in a literal sense. Dostoevsky tells us that Zossima is about to rise from the earth, but in the form of Alyosha, the monk in the world. There is a kind of miracle of resurrection after all.

The biblical image associated with Alyosha's conversion is not resurrection, however, but the first Johannine sign, the miracle at Cana—the very passage Father Paissy had been reading over Zossima's body just before Alyosha left the elder's cell.

The vault of heaven, studded with softly shining stars, stretched wide and vast over him. From the zenith to the horizon the

Milky Way stretched its two arms dimly across the sky. The fresh, motionless, still night enfolded the earth. The white towers and golden domes of the cathedral gleamed against the sapphire sky. The gorgeous autumn flowers in the beds near the house went to sleep till morning. The silence of the earth seemed to merge into the silence of the heavens, the mystery of the earth came in contact with the mystery of the stars. . . . Alyosha stood, gazed, and suddenly he threw himself down flat, upon the earth.

He did not know why he was embracing it. He could not have explained to himself why he longed so irresistibly to kiss it, to kiss it all, but he kissed it weeping, sobbing and drenching it with his tears, and vowed frenziedly to love it, to love it for ever and ever. "Water the earth with the tears of your gladness and love those tears," it rang in his soul. What was he weeping over? Oh, he was weeping in his rapture even over those stars which were shining for him from the abyss of space and "he was not ashamed of that ecstasy." It was as though the threads from all those innumerable worlds of God met all at once in his soul, and it was trembling all over "as it came in contact with other worlds." He wanted to forgive everyone and for everything, and to beg forgiveness—oh! not for himself, but for all men, for all and for everything, "and others are begging it for me," it echoed in his soul again. But with every moment he felt clearly and almost palpably that something firm and immovable, like the firmament itself, was entering his soul. A sort of idea was gaining an ascendancy over his mind—and that for the rest of his life, for ever and ever. He had fallen upon the earth a weak youth, but he rose from it a resolute fighter for the rest of his life, and he realized and felt it suddenly, at the very moment of his rapture. (pp. 426-27)

Is this a Christian experience? It is a conversion, no doubt, but to what? There is a resurrection theme, but it has a pantheistic and humanistic tinge, as does the resurrection language at the end of the novel. It is a union with the earth, this much is clear. Why does Dostoevsky call this scene "Cana in Galilee," where Jesus performed the very unspiritual act of changing water into wine at a wedding-party? Berdyaev assumes that this is a Christian conversion and comments:

Thus did Dostoevsky bring man's wanderings to a close: when he is separated from nature and earth he is cast into hell, at the end of his course he comes back to them. But there is no such return for him who is wedded to self-will and rebellion, it is possible only by way of Cana and Jesus Christ. The return is to a transfigured nature and a transfigured earth; the old nature and earth are closed to the man who has known self-will and inner division; there is no recovering a lost Eden, he must seek a new one.

This is eloquent, but irrelevant to the passage at hand, and the suggestion that the man of self-will (Ivan) is shut off from hope is clearly not what Dostoevsky says. Martin Jarrett-Kerr in his *Studies in Literature and Belief* also sees this scene as a Christian conversion. He cites the rites of prostration and kissing in the Orthodox liturgy, and notes the number of times the kiss is a symbol of acceptance and forgiveness in the novel: Zossima at the foot of Dmitry, Christ and the Inquisitor. Is the kiss of the earth here really forgiveness and acceptance? Dostoevsky insists in the passage that Alyosha himself does not ask for forgiveness. Why? Doesn't he need it? Doesn't he deserve it? What does it mean to say that Alyosha accepts the earth? Is the earth here God's creation; is it the earth that refused to give back Zossima by means of a foolish miracle? Perhaps, but the earth is first a symbol of fertility and sensuality. Alyosha's kiss of the earth is not so much a sacramental act uniting the physical and spiritual as it is a sign of the victory of the Karamazov strain in him: the earth-bound force, unrestrained and crude, as Father Paissy had put it. Is this not really a conversion to a spiritualized sensuality, a victory of the Karamazovs over Zossima? The child of grace will still be his father's son, after all. We are told that Alyosha rose a resolute fighter. But a fighter for what? In the rest of the novel he is no fighter. He seems, if anything, even more ineffectual than before. Just what is the content of Alyosha's faith?

It is to be identified with Zossima's faith, for Alyosha is intended to be a Zossima in the making and in the world. It is also doubtless to be identified with what Dostoevsky longed for but did not have. Dostoevsky was perhaps drawn to Dmitry's way, to Ivan's way, and to Alyosha's way; each is the object of his desire. In any case, Alyosha's vision proceeds from Zossima's words about love and the earth, and especially from:

> Don't say, the power of evil, of the wicked world, is great, but we, we are guiltless. . . . We are responsible to all for all, apart from our own sins. It's only that men don't know it. . . . Each man is part of the single organism of all humanity, and every one of us accordingly shares the guilt for every crime, for everything that happens on earth. (p. 377)

What is most striking about Alyosha is his love of humanity, his faith in people, in all people (pp. 16, 17, 821). The new man that Dostoevsky sees emerging in Alyosha is a communal man, bound to his brothers in a new kind of community. Perhaps Alyosha's views were suggested by the ideas of Solovyev (who published his lectures on Godmanhood in 1881), and if so, this would point to a Christian source for Zossima's teaching and Alyosha's vision of a new humanity. But Ivanov's words seem more accurate. He calls Alyosha "a philanthropist of religious tendency." The community of this vision is more like the nation than the church, though there is some evidence that Dostoevsky himself longed for a transformed nation that would be merged into the national church. The first mark of this new community is the brotherhood of boys that is mentioned at the very end of the novel, banding together in loyalty to the memory of Ilyusha (pp. 910-13). But is this vision of a common humanity, confessing its solidarity in suffering and joy, really a new insight?

That there is a vision of something is clear. It is a vision that points toward the highest possible development of man on earth, through an affirmation of life, goodness and beauty. Dostoevsky once said that "beauty will save the world." This vision indeed led Dostoevsky to turn against both the new bourgeoisie and the positivists and socialists in the Russia of his day. But surely it is related only verbally to a Christian understanding of life. Philip Rahv may well be right to call this vision "little more than an anarcho-Christian version of that 'religion of humanity' which continued to inspire the intelligentsia throughout the nineteenth century and by which Dostoevsky himself was inspired in his youth."

> The teaching of Alyosha (writes D. A. Traversi) hardly contains a word of the Incarnation. . . . It is a purely personal mysticism, often using Christian terminology, but rather sentimental and pantheistic in its force. It lays stress upon "watering the earth with your tears," but the reader is troubled by lack of feeling for the real earth of creation; Dostoevsky's earth is merely there to be wept upon. His lack of sympathy for the sensible and the tangible lands him finally in sentimental weakness.

Is there not, once more, a fatal lack of clarity about Alyosha? What was the earth he fell upon, and what did he rise up to do? Is the new humanity which he seems to embody to be founded on Comte or on Christ? And if on Christ, whose picture of Christ? Here is how Middleton Murry in his book on Dostoevsky concludes his interpretation of the novel:

> The present age is ended in suffering and gloom; from its loins springs forth the new harmony. Alyosha is a perfect being in body, and his mind is in harmony with his body's perfection. He, the actual Alyosha, is only a symbol of what is to come. . . . This Alyosha, the resolute champion, is not a Christian. He has passed beyond the Christian revelation. . . . He may not believe in God, he may know himself for a sensualist, yet he is not confounded, for his knowledge of the great Oneness needs no belief in God for its support.

There is something odd and curious about Dostoevsky's view of God. In the Inquisitor legend, he seems to believe in a sort of Christ figure, but one whose roots are more in popular Orthodox piety than in tradition or scripture, and, as we have seen, there is no God behind or above this Christ. The Christ of the legend comes from nowhere and goes nowhere. But if there is no God behind this Christ, there is a God for Dostoevsky. It can be described, but it is hard to relate it to the Christ of the legend. Stefan Zweig, in his book *Master Builders,* says:

For Dostoevsky, God is the principle of unrest; He is the primal father of contrasts, simultaneously the affirmative and the negative. . . . Dostoevsky's God is not the benevolent and venerable ancient depicted by the old masters, nor is he the gentle spirit. . . . He is, rather . . . not a being but a condition, a condition of tension, a process whereby the emotions are consumed; he is a fire, a flame, heating men to the point of ecstasy. He is a lash, scourging them out of their warm, calm bodies into infinity; he lures them to every excess whether of word or deed, and hurls them into the burning bush of vice. He resembles the men who are his creatures, the men who created him, for He is an insatiable God, whom no exertion can master, no thought fully grasp, no sacrifice content. He is the everlasting unattainable, the pain of pains. . . .

The ethical significance of Dostoevsky's work is a delicate subject, for it is hard to separate what we know of the man from his teaching. Turgenev called Dostoevsky "the most evil Christian I have ever met in my life." The critic Strakhov once wrote in a letter to Tolstoy: "I cannot consider Dostoevsky either a good or happy man. He was wicked, envious, vicious, and he spent the whole of his life in emotions and irritations which would have made him pitiable, even ridiculous, had he not been so wicked and so intelligent." André Gide grants all this, but claims that Dostoevsky's submission to Christ held the discordant elements in his personality together. Do we have enough evidence to decide such a matter? Does Dostoevsky overcome his own immorality, or is it merely sublimated in his artistic creations? Freud's indictment in his essay "Dostoevsky and Parricide" is hard:

The moralist in Dostoevsky is the most readily assailable. If we rank him high as a moralist on the plea that only a man who has gone through the depths of sin can reach the highest heights of morality, we are neglecting one consideration. A moral man is one who reacts to the temptation he feels in his heart without yielding to it. The man who alternately sins, and in his remorse makes high moral demands, lays himself open to the reproach that he has made things too easy for himself. He has not achieved the most important thing in morality, renunciation, for the moral conduct of life is a practical human interest.

There is no denying Dostoevsky's prophetic powers, but his answers are fatally confused. He bequeaths at once deep insight and inner division. Not even Zossima and Alyosha provide a clear moral guide. Out of his moral tension, he proposed a vague populism and a quietistic "sort of Buddhism," as Gide called it, that tries to love all things without facing the fact that we can only love particulars.

Dostoevsky is important because he can and does teach us how in fact we do believe, for he has understood, as only a great artist can, the struggle between belief and unbelief.

Dostoevsky began as an atheist and a revolutionary in his twenties, and before his exile into Siberia he had been a profound explorer of the underground depths of man's nature. While in Siberia he was converted to a sort of mystical populist faith which ultimately came to be directed toward the Russian people as bearers of God, a nation-church. The twin strands of belief and unbelief were always together in him, and it seems as if he never really rid himself of either. In a letter to a friend he wrote:

> As far as I am concerned, I look upon myself as a child of the age, a child of unbelief and doubt; it is probable, nay I know for certain, that I shall remain so to my dying day. I have been tortured with longing to believe—am so, indeed, even now; and the yearning grows stronger, the more cogent the intellectual difficulties that stand in the way.

Yet, in the same letter, he continues,

> And yet God sometimes sends me moments of complete serenity. It is in such moments that I have composed in my mind a profession of faith, in which everything is clear and holy. This profession of faith is very simple. This is what it is: to believe that there is nothing finer, deeper, more lovable, more reasonable, braver and more perfect than Christ; and, not only there is nothing, but, I tell myself with a jealous love, there cannot

be anything. More than that: if anyone had told me that Christ is outside truth, and if it had really been established that truth is outside Christ, I should have preferred to stay with Christ rather than with truth.

Thurneysen is fully at ease with this paradoxical tension, as he of course calls it. Unbelief seems like the last word, he says, but it is not:

Something has happened, something has taken place; the questionableness of everything human has been revealed and accentuated, and the riddle of existence cries out even more tragically for its ultimate solution in God.

Beyond the cry of unbelief and the agony of human need, however, is the reality of God himself.

Therefore, the final word describing the true meaning of existence is not (in Dostoevsky) a problematic word. . . . What is impossible with men is possible with God. If no steps lead from us to Him, certainly steps will lead from Him to us. Revelation is being preached here. The eschatological tension becomes eschatology itself with Dostoevsky. The final word of his novel is resurrection. Above the dark abyss of humanity shines the eternal light of a great forgiveness.[12]

To the theologian this suggests Barth's *Romans*, and it would be nice to have Dostoevsky so neatly in our midst. But a close examination of the novel makes it impossible to believe even in this sophisticated eschatological victory for faith.

In fact Dostoevsky was both a convinced atheist and a convinced believer. It doesn't even help much to say that he denied God and affirmed Christ, because in place of the denied God he put his own passionate Karamazov God; and, as we have seen, the Christ he affirmed is a strange and elusive combination of a principle of freedom, an ugly Russian ikon, and a suffering nation. He believed that salvation and peace come only by renunciation of the self, but he also believed that man

[12] Thurneysen, *op. cit.*, p. 39. Previous citation from p. 38.

is never closer to God than in his extremity of self-conscious despair.

The mixture is further complicated by the fact that his unbelieving side found itself preaching the need for unbelief, not out of arrogance, but out of compassion, lest all men suffer under God as he had done. Freud remarks that Dostoevsky was unable to shake himself free from faith because of his strongly developed feelings of guilt. Such feelings, Freud says, are often the unconscious basis for faith, and they were too strong in Dostoevsky to be overcome by his mind that saw the evidence against God so clearly. "God is necessary and must exist"; and, at the same time, "I know he doesn't and cannot." This tension is almost inevitable because of the terrible transcendence of Dostoevsky's God, too transcendent to stoop to an Incarnation, unrelated to man, approachable only by an extreme denial of nature and sense. That is why, as Traversi says, Dostoevsky's hero-mystics are driven by their thirst for this God "into straining the boundaries of human experience, so that their ecstasy inevitably coincides with the dissolution of the personality into epileptic idiocy."

Yet, at the close of his life, while engaged in writing *The Brothers Karamazov,* Dostoevsky seemed to believe that he broke through his doubt into a kind of faith. He wrote in his diary, after the first criticisms of the early installments of the novel began to appear:

> The dolts have ridiculed my obscurantism and the reactionary character of my faith. These fools could not even conceive so strong a denial of God as the one to which I gave expression (in the novel). . . . The whole book is an answer to *that.* You might search Europe in vain for so powerful an expression of atheism. Thus it is not like a child that I believe in Christ and confess Him. My hosanna has come forth from the crucible of doubt.

It is terrible not to be able to believe Dostoevsky's own words, at the close of his life, but the evidence of the novel does not quite bear out the claim he makes. Thus, as Stefan Zweig says:

At one and the same time he is the truest of believers and the most arrant atheist; these polar extremes are convincingly portrayed in the characters of his novels, though he himself remained unconvinced and undecided; we are shown, on the one hand, abject humility and the craving to become absorbed into the divine essence, and, on the other, the magnificent pride of being God oneself. He loves both the servant of God and the the man who denies God, both Alyosha and Ivan. . . . His faith oscillates between Yea and Nay, the two poles of the universe. In the very presence of God, Dostoevsky remains banished from the land of unity.

But perhaps Dostoevsky's claim and our protest are both right in their own way. The faith that comes from the crucible of doubt is certainly Alyosha, and it was he whom Dostoevsky thought to be the key to the new man and the new belief. But something has gone wrong so that Alyosha cannot be the answer. If Dostoevsky himself was unclear and vague it may be that, after all, the trouble is with us and not Dostoevsky. My objections may only mean that it is possible for us to receive only part of Dostoevsky's religious vision today. Perhaps he seems to be "banished from the land of unity" because we are the truly banished ones.

My conclusion would be that we ought not to trust ourselves to claim that we have Dostoevsky's final secret. But whether it be Dostoevsky's unclarity or our blindness that makes us unable to receive Alyosha, we can all receive Ivan with a terrible kind of delight. Here is a true gift to us all, perhaps Dostoevsky's supreme gift. Ivan's picture of himself we immediately recognize as self-portrait; the God that is dead for him is dead for us; and his Karamazov-God of tension and terror is often the only one we are able to find.

Ivan does not tell us how to live or how to believe, but he does tell us how in fact we do believe. Is it, then, that we are fated to go the way he went? Is clarity and certain faith only an eschatological vision, the reality of which can never be enjoyed now?

W. H.

If a certain heady mixture of Ivan Karamazov and Dietrich Bonhoeffer provided the inner materials for the move into radical theology, a modest request and then later a general series of encouragements from Professor Hugh T. Kerr, Jr., of Princeton Theological Seminary and Theology Today provided the external occasion to move the radical theology out of the realm of interior monologue, letters with friends, and the obscurity of learned journals. This essay is not wholly autobiographical. The device of the ambivalent narrator works better in the novel than in the theological article, but I wanted to keep the reader off guard by having him argue not with me, which is easy, but with a series of moods and happenings. The response was sufficient to suggest further investigation and refinement. I cannot avoid paying tribute to Tim Kerr both as editor and friend who seemed to know when I was tempted to blow uncertain sounds and who always talked me out of it.

W. H.

Thursday's Child

Non-theological observers have been saying for some time that America is a place and a people without a past and without a future, or, more exactly, without a sense of having a past and without a sense of being able to count on a stable future. America is the place that has travelled farthest along the road from the cloister to the world that Luther and the Reformation mapped out. We are the most profane, the most banal, the most utterly worldly of places. Western Europe is positively numinous with divine substance compared to us, and even the Communist world has a kind of spiritual substance and vitality that we are said to lack. Both the academic sabbatical leave and the conventional summer vacation bear witness to the American's need to go abroad to look for something he has not found at home.

Hope is the way of declaring one's future to be open and assured, and love is the way of standing before your neighbor in the present moment. Taking faith, hope and love together, the feeling is that the American theologian can really live in only one of them at a time, perhaps only one in a lifetime. If this is so, and if it is also so that as an American he is fated to be a man without a sense of past or future, then it follows that the theologian today and tomorrow is a man without faith, without hope, with only the present, with only love to guide him.

I propose that we should not only acknowledge, but will this faithlessness. What does it mean to say that the theologian in America is a man without faith? Is he therefore a man without God? It would seem to follow. He has his doctrine of God, several of them no doubt, and all correct. But that is surely not the point. He really doesn't believe in God, or that there is a God, or that God exists. It is not that he is fashionably against idols or opposed to God as a Being or as part of the world. It is God himself he has trouble with. Can one stand before God in unbelief? In what sense is such a man "before God"? Faith, or trusting in God, ought to produce some palpable fruits. The theologian may sometimes see these, but never in himself. Something has happened. At the center of his thoughts and meditations is a void, a disappearance, an absence. It is sometimes said that only a wounded physician can heal.

Other pertinent questions can be raised. Does the theologian go to church? The answer is "no." He may, in the past, have concealed this "no" from himself by escaping into church work, speaking to church groups, preaching at church or college, slaking his thirst for worship and word in more protected communities. But now he is facing up to this banal answer to the banal question, and he wills to say "no" openly.

It used to be otherwise. In the past, the theologian would distinguish between God, Christendom, Christianity and church, so that a different balance of "yes" and "no" could be uttered to each. Now he finds himself equally alienated from each of the realities represented by the four terms, and he says his "no" to each.

The quality of the theologian's "no" to the church differs from the impressive, if verbose, debate now being waged by the church's sociological pundits. In this debate the issue is drawn between a kind of strident despair and a grim hope. The theologian, however, is neither despairing nor hopeful about the church. He is not interested, and he no longer has the energy or interest to answer ecclesiastical questions about What the Church Must Do to Revitalize Itself. One can choose his own language here: the theologian does not and can not go to church, he is not interested, he is alienated (for a tenser word), he must live outside. He is not thereby a happier man, nor is he a troubled one. He is neither proud nor guilty. He has just decided that this is how it has to be, and he has decided to say so.

Does our theologian write books in systematic theology? That is, does he sit down and decide that he'd better do a theological book? The answer is a clear "no." First he gets his doctoral dissertation published. If it is any good, he can get quite a few years of professional mileage from it, defending it, clarifying, writing articles on relevant new material. From then on he speaks and writes as he is asked. Editors, ecclesiastics, institutions and other scholars assign him subjects they think he would be interested in. In this way he can get a reputation for being skilled and interested in a field in which he has no interest whatever. As the years pass, the gulf between what he wants to do and what he does grows wider. His books, if any, are either private love-letters (or hate-letters) to fellow guild members or lecture series that offer an extra five hundred dollars for publication. Anything serious he manages will probably appear in articles.

What does the theologian read? Does he read religious books in hardcovers? Less and less, perhaps not at all, except when he has a free copy for a review or a bibliography to prepare. He has been unable to read books of sermons for a long time, and he has recently found that he practically never reads a book of theology for the sheer fun of it. He reads a lot of paperbacks, articles and reviews. Just as less and less theological writing is being put into books, the theological reader is reading fewer and fewer books. One wonders quite seriously if there is any long-range future for hardcover religious book publishing, apart from church materials, reference works and perhaps text books.

Is the theologian reading the Bible? Of course, he is forced into a kind of affable semi-professional relationship with Scripture in his daily work. But what has gone is the rigorous systematic confronting of Scripture, expecting the Word of God to be made manifest when one approaches it with faith or at least with a broken and contrite heart. Perhaps because he is without either faith or the truly contrite heart, the Bible is a strange book that does not come alive to him as it is supposed to. There are still some pieces of it that come alive, to be sure, although he is not sure why or how: this psalmist, that prophetic call, a piece or two of Job, perhaps even some words of Jesus.

The theologian is alienated from the Bible, just as he is alienated from God and the church. This alienation may not last. If it doesn't last, fine; if it does last, the theologian will have some piercing questions to ask of himself. But there are wrong ways (Karl Barth) and right ways to overcome this alienation, and for now he has to be honest with himself, with the God before whom he stands in unbelief, and he must wait.

Given this state of affairs, what is this theologian really like? How does he act? Is he consciously or unconsciously dishonest? What is the relation between his public and private persona? The theologian can be exonerated from certain coarse professional faults: he is not overly ambitious for position or even notice; he is not moving in this direction so that he can be seen by men or because of some special delight he has *épater le bourgeoisie.* Like all men, he lives in a public and in a private sphere, and like most men he works hard to keep the first from overpowering the second. On his public and professional side he is likely to make use of two different masks. One is modestly devout, earnest and serious, one which he uses for his teaching and church work. The other is a modestly worldly mask for his non-religious friends and for the forms of their common life. Sometimes he deliberately decides to interchange the masks, and wears the worldly mask for a church talk, a lecture, or even a sermon here or there. This leads to some harmless fun, and he is careful to see that everybody enjoys himself. Sometimes he dons the devout mask for his worldly friends and their parties, and this too is quite harmless, for his friends understand and sometimes even admire his willingness to stand up for his odd beliefs.

But back in the private realm, he is coming more and more to distrust this kind of manipulation. God—this much he knows —is no respecter of persons or personae or masks, and the theologian really knows that he is neither mask. He knows that his rebellion and unbelief is both deeper and uglier than his bland worldly mask suggests, and he knows also (a bit less assuredly?) that his devout mask is too vapid. To be a man of two masks is, he knows, to be less than honest. Thus, he has had to come out into the open about his faithlessness even though he may suspect and hope that beneath it is a passion and a genuine waiting for something that may, one day, get transformed into a kind of faith even better than the one he has willed to lose.

Is this theologian alone, or does he live in a community that needs and nourishes him? He is not alone, but he does not ordinarily live in a true community, though he is aware of the existence of such a community. He rarely gets close enough to anybody to identify him as a member of this community, but he knows that there is no place under the sun where a member of this community may not be found. They may, of course, even be found in the church.

The problem is not, as might be suspected, that he has no doctrine of the church; it is with the doctrine of the church that he does have his problem. Professionally he finds himself working with three quite different understandings of the church, but only the third makes genuine sense to him and it is far too imprecise to be very helpful.

The first understanding of the church states that it is to be defined by the classical marks of the church—unity, holiness, catholicity, apostolicity. In his ecumenical work or in the emerging Roman Catholic-Protestant dialogue, he is compelled to see the church in this way. The second way reminds him that the church is found where the word of God is preached and the sacraments rightly administered. This doctrine of the church is most congenial to his own theology and theological vocation. He has always been drawn to a theology of the Word, and he has had moments when he has felt that theology might, after all, be able to minister to the church's proclamation.

But somehow he has had to come to define the church in a third way. The church is present whenever Christ is being formed among men in the world. This is a very vague way of describing his feelings about the community, even though it has no outlines, no preaching, sacraments or liturgy.

One final question needs to be asked: What is the theologian doing now? The answer comes in two parts, the first related to what we have called his loss of God, of faith, of the church. In the face of all this, he is a passive man, trusting in waiting, silence, and in a kind of prayer for the losses to be returned. He does not do this anxiously, nor does he seem a particularly broken or troubled sort of person. If it is true that he is somehow without hope as well as without faith, he is not in despair about himself. His waiting is more docile and patient and has little existential moodiness in it. There is, of course, no single Christian doctrine which he affirms or grasps with guileless joy, but for all of his acute sense of loss, he has an overwhelmingly positive sense of being in and not out; even in his unbelief he is somehow home and not in a far country. He would say, for example: "As long as the Gethsemane prayer stands there somehow close to the center of things, I can stand there. If it should have to go, I might have to go too."

The theologian today is thus both a waiting man and a praying man. His faith and hope may be badly flawed, but his love is not. It is not necessary to probe the cultural, psychological, or even marital reasons for this, but simply to note it as a fact. In Christology, the theologian is sometimes inclined to suspect that Jesus Christ is best understood as neither the object nor the ground of faith, neither as person, event or community, but simply as a place to be, a standpoint. That place is, of course, alongside the neighbor, being for him. This may be the meaning of Jesus' true humanity and it may even be the meaning of his divinity, and thus of divinity itself. In any case, now—even when he knows so little about what to believe —he does know where to be. Today, for example, he is with the Negro community in its struggle (he will work out his own understanding of what "being with" must mean for him), working and watching, not yet evangelizing. He is also with all sorts of other groups: poets and critics, psychiatrists and physicists and philosophers. He is not in these places primarily to make things happen—a new solution to the science-religion problem

or a new theological literary criticism—but just to be himself
and to be attentive, as a man and therefore as a theologian.
This is what his form of love looks like. It is a love that takes
place in the middle of the real world, the ugly, banal, godless,
religious world of America today.

He has been drawn, then, to these worldly places by love
(not by apologetics or evangelism), and it is his hope that in
such places his faithlessness and dishonesty may be broken.
His love is not a secure and confident one, and thus it is not
condescending. It is not, therefore, what some men call *agape*.
It is a broken love, one that is needy and weak. It is thus a little
like what men call *eros*. To be sure, his whole project may be
swept away in a moment, if it can be shown that the theologian
is just fleeing from one kind of religion-as-need-fulfillment to
another. Perhaps someone will be able to show him that his
weak and needy love has some points of connection with the
love of the Cross.

Dietrich Bonhoeffer is, of course, deeply involved in this
portrait. Have we discovered this in him, and then in ourselves;
or in ourselves, and then rejoiced to find it in him? I think
the second is nearer the truth. In any case, as Western Europe
turns away from Bonhoeffer as a theological mentor, we in
America can welcome his fragmentary help.

> Atonement and redemption, regeneration, the Holy Ghost, the
> love of our enemies, the cross of resurrection, life in Christ and
> Christian discipleship—all these things have become so proble-
> matic and so remote that we hardly dare any more to speak of
> them. . . . So our traditional language must perforce become
> powerless and remain silent, and our Christianity today will be
> confined to praying for and doing right by our fellow men.
> Christian thinking, speaking, and organization must be reborn
> out of this praying and this action.*

W. H.

* Dietrich Bonhoeffer, "Thoughts on the Baptism of D. W. R.,"
Letters and Papers from Prison, pp. 187-88 in the 1962 paperback edition,
The Macmillan Company.

*Shortly after finishing "America and the Future of Theology,"
I took up a task which had somewhat earlier been assigned me
by Herbert Weisinger, editor of* The Centennial Review.
*He had decided to devote an issue of this journal, with my
collaboration, to the topic: "The Crisis in Crisis Theology."
I wanted to write something that would both meet his
assignment and not collapse under his critical eye, and at
the same time be a step ahead in my own work.*

T. J. J. A.

Theology and the Death of God

Contemporary theology is unquestionably in a state of crisis, perhaps the most profound crisis which Christian theology has faced since its creation. This crisis is manifest in three areas: (1) in the relation of dogmatic theology to its biblical ground, a crisis posed by the rise of modern historical understanding; (2) in the relation of theology to the sensibility and *Existenz* of contemporary man, a crisis created by the death of God; and (3) in the relation of the community of faith to the whole order of social, political and economic institutions, a crisis initiated by the collapse of Christendom. I intend to focus upon the second of these areas, although it can only be artificially isolated from the other two. Furthermore, we shall simply assume the truth of Nietzsche's proclamation of the death of God, a truth which has thus far been ignored or set aside by contemporary theology. This means that we shall understand the death of God as an historical event: God has died in *our* time, in *our* history, in *our* existence. The man who chooses to live in our destiny can neither know the reality of God's presence nor understand the world as his creation; or, at least, he can no longer respond—either interiorly or cognitively—to the classical Christian images of the Creator and the creation. In this situation, an affirmation of the traditional forms of faith becomes a Gnostic escape from the brute realities of history.

Modern theology, as we shall understand it, was founded by Sören Kierkegaard; and founded not simply in response to the collapse of Christendom, but more deeply in response to the advent of a reality that was wholly divorced from the world of faith, or, as Kierkegaard saw, a reality that was created by the negation of faith. While employing the Hegelian categories of the "universal" and the "objective" as a means of understanding the new reality created by modern man, Kierkegaard came to understand the modern consciousness as the product of a Faustian choice. Modern philosophy is, as Kierkegaard argued in *The Sickness Unto Death,* simply paganism, its real secret being: "*cogito ergo sum,* to think is to be"; whereas the Christian motto, on the contrary, is: "As thou believest, so art thou; to believe is to be." Here, *cogito* and *credo* are antithetical acts: modern or "objective" knowledge is not religiously neutral, as so many theologians have imagined; rather, it is grounded in a dialectical negation of faith. Again, to know "objectively" is to exist "objectively," and such existence is the antithetical opposite of the "subjectivity" which Kierkegaard identified as faith. With the birth of objective knowledge, reality appeared as an objective order, and God was banished from the "real" world. But for Kierkegaard, who was living at a moment when a Christian sensibility was still a possibility, it was not only God but also the concretely existing individual who was banished from the world of the "universal." Already, in *Fear and Trembling,* the major theme of the "knight of faith" is threatened by the minor theme that ". . . the individual is incommensurable with reality," that ". . . subjectivity is incommensurable with reality." So radical is this incommensurability that the existing individual and objective reality now exist in a state of dialectical opposition: to know objectively is to cease to exist subjectively, to exist subjectively is to cease to know objectively. Moreover, it was precisely Kierkegaard's realization of the radically profane ground of modern knowledge that made possible his creation of a modern Christian mode of dialectical understanding. Existence in faith is antithetically related to existence in objective reality; now faith becomes subjective, momentary and paradoxical. In short, existence in faith is existence by virtue of the absurd. Why the absurd? Because faith is antithetically related to "objectivity." Therefore true faith is radical inwardness or subjectivity, it comes into existence by a negation of objectivity, and can only maintain itself by a continual process, or repetition, of *negating* objectivity.

Kierkegaard's dialectical method is fully presented in the *Postscript,* but it was a method which was destined never to be fully evolved. Quite simply the reason why this method never reached completion is that it never—despite his initial effort in *Fear and Trembling*—moved beyond the level of negation. Although biographically Kierkegaard's choice of a negative dialectic was hardened by his second conversion or "metamorphosis," a conversion which led to his resolve to attack the established church, and hence to abandon philosophy, it is also true that he could limit faith to a negative dialectical movement because he could identify faith and "subjectivity." In the *Postscript,* subjective thinking is "existential," and ". . . passion is the culmination of existence for an existing individual." But "passion" is radical inwardness, and true inwardness is "eternity" (an identification first established in *The Concept of Dread*). To be sure, "eternity" is a subjective and not an objective category, and therefore it can only be reached through inwardness. Nevertheless, the crucial point is that Kierkegaard could identify authentic human existence with existence in faith. Kierkegaard knew the death of God only as an objective reality; indeed, it was "objectivity" that was created by the death of God. Accordingly, faith is made possible by the negation of objectivity, and since "objectivity" and "subjectivity" are antithetical categories, it follows that faith can be identified with "subjectivity." Today we can see that Kierkegaard could dialectically limit "objectivity" and "subjectivity" to the level of antithetical categories because he still lived in an historical time when subjectivity could be known as indubitably Christian. Less than a hundred years later, it will be little less than blasphemy to identify the truly "existential" with existence in faith. But in Kierkegaard's time the death of God had not yet become a subjective reality. Hence authentic human existence could be understood as culminating in faith, the movement of faith could be limited to the negation of "objectivity," and no occasion need arise for the necessity of a dialectical coincidence of the opposites. Yet no dialectical method can be complete until it leads to this final *coincidentia oppositorum*.

11

If radical dialectical thinking was reborn in Kierkegaard, it was consummated in Friedrich Nietzsche: the thinker who, in Martin Heidegger's words, brought to an end the metaphysical tradition of the West. Nietzsche's proclamation of the death of God shattered the transcendence of Being. No longer is there a metaphysical hierarchy or order which can give meaning or value to existing beings (*Seiendes*); as Heidegger points out, now there is no *Sein* of *Seiendes*. Nietzsche was, of course, a prophetic thinker, which means that his thought reflected the deepest reality of his time, and of our time as well; for to exist in our time is to exist in what Sartre calls a "hole in Being," a "hole" created by the death of God. However, the proclamation of the death of God—or, more deeply, the *willing* of the death of God—is dialectical: a No-saying to God (the transcendence of *Sein*) makes possible a Yes-saying to human existence (*Dasein*, total existence in the *here* and *now*). Absolute transcendence is transformed into absolute immanence; being *here* and *now* (the post-Christian existential "now") draws into itself all those powers which were once bestowed upon the Beyond. Consequently, Nietzsche's vision of Eternal Recurrence is the dialectical correlate of his proclamation of the death of God.

> Everything goes, everything comes back; eternally rolls the wheel of being. Everything dies, everything blossoms again; eternally runs the year of being. Everything breaks, everything is joined anew; eternally the same house of being is built. Everything parts, everything greets every other thing again; eternally the ring of being remains faithful to itself. In every Now, being begins; round every Here rolls the sphere There. The center is everywhere. Bent is the path of eternity. (*Also Sprach Zarathustra*, Part III)

Only when God is dead can Being begin in every Now. Eternal Recurrence is neither a cosmology nor a metaphysical idea: it is Nietzsche's symbol of the deepest affirmation of existence, of Yes-saying. Accordingly, Eternal Recurrence is a symbolic portrait of the truly contemporary man, the man who dares to live in *our* time, in *our* history, in *our* existence.

We must observe that Eternal Recurrence is a dialectical inversion of the biblical category of the Kingdom of God. Jesus' proclamation of the Kingdom of God makes incarnate a transcendent Wholly Other, a Wholly Other that radically reverses the believer's existence in both the being and the values of the Old Aeon of history, and makes possible even now a participation in the New Aeon of grace. So likewise the "existential" truth of Eternal Recurrence shatters the power of the old order of history, transforming transcendence into immanence, and thereby making eternity incarnate in every Now. Eternal Recurrence is the dialectical antithesis of the Christian God. The creature becomes the Creator when the Center is everywhere. Hence Zarathustra, the proclaimer of Eternal Recurrence, is the first "immoralist," and his proclamation is a product of the "second innocence" of atheism. The atheistic Nietzsche was the enemy of God and Christ. But Nietzsche was a dialectical thinker. His opposition to Christ was directed against the Christ of Christianity, against religion itself, rather than against the actual figure of Jesus. Again and again, in *The Antichrist,* Nietzsche portrays Jesus as a kind of naive forerunner of Zarathustra. For Jesus is incapable of resentment (non-dialectical negation), is liberated from "history," and is himself the exact opposite of Christianity. For, as Nietzsche says:

> If one were to look for signs that an ironical divinity has its fingers in the great play of the world, one would find no small support in the *tremendous question mark* called Christianity. Mankind lies on its knees before the opposite of that which was the origin, the meaning, the *right* of the evangel; in the concept of "church" it has pronounced holy precisely what the "bringer of the glad tidings" felt to be *beneath* and *behind* himself—one would look in vain for a greater example of *world-historical irony.*

Jesus' proclamation abolishes any distance separating God and man (a distance which religion knows as sin). His gospel did not promise blessedness, nor did it bind salvation to legal or moral conditions: blessedness is the "only reality." What Christianity has called the gospel is actually the opposite of that which Jesus lived: "*ill* tidings, a *dysangel*." Christianity is a *dysangel* because it retreated into the very "history" which Jesus transcended and transformed, the transformation of the blessedness of Jesus' proclamation into the No-saying of resentment. Thus Nietzsche looked upon Christianity as the stone upon the grave of Jesus.

The astute theological student of Nietzsche must wonder whether Nietzsche's portrait of Zarathustra is not a modern dialectical image of Jesus. Not the "Christian" Jesus to be sure, but already the modern Christian has lived through the death of historical or objective Christianity in Kierkegaard's realization of faith as radical subjectivity. If Kierkegaard's subjectivity has dialectically passed into Nietzsche's Eternal Recurrence, is it possible that the radically profane Now of Eternal Recurrence is a dialectical resurrection of a Kingdom of God beyond God? Does not the New Creation (Eternal Recurrence) of Zarathustra parallel the New Creation of Jesus (the Kingdom of God) insofar as it shatters history, dissolves all rational meaning, and brings to an end the rule of Law? Such a radically modern *coincidentia oppositorum* would parallel the highest expressions of mysticism (*e.g.*, the Madhyamika and Zen schools of Mahayana Buddhism) while at the same time offering a non-Gnostic form of faith. Non-Gnostic because a truly modern dialectical form of faith would meet the actual historical destiny of contemporary man while yet transforming his unique *Existenz* into the purity of eschatological faith. In Nietzsche, we have witnessed the deepest willing of the death of God pass into the deepest affirmation of Eternal Recurrence. Dialectically, the opposites coincide, radical negation has become radical affirmation; but if the negative movement is a denial of God, then the positive movement must finally be an affirmation of God, of the God beyond the Christian God, beyond the God of the historic Church, beyond all which Christendom has known as God. A truly dialectical image of God (or of the Kingdom of God) will appear only after the most radical negation, just as a genuinely eschatological form of faith can now be reborn only upon the grave of the God who is the symbol of the transcendence of Being. Does Nietzsche point the way to a form of faith that will be authentically contemporary and eschatological at once?

III

We shall define eschatological faith as a form of faith that calls the believer out of his old life in history and into a new Reality of grace. This Reality (the Kingdom of God) effects a radical transformation of the reality of the world, reversing both its forms and structures, a transformation that must finally culminate in the "end" of the world. Historically, eschatological faith was born in the reform prophetic movement of the Old Testament prophets, at a time when the world of ancient Israel was crumbling. In all probability, the prophetic oracles recording this revolutionary eschatological faith did not assume either a written or a canonical form until the Jewish Exile or thereafter. Moreover, it was not until the time of Jesus that a fully eschatological form of faith appeared, for only in Jesus' proclamations does the Kingdom of God cease to be a promise and become instead a present reality. As Rudolf Otto notes in *The Kingdom of God and the Son of Man,* the idea which was entirely unique and peculiar to Jesus was ". . . that the Kingdom—supramundane, future, and belonging to a new era—penetrated from the future into the present, from its place in the beyond into this order, and was operative redemptively as a divine power, as an inbreaking realm of salvation." However, the power of the Kingdom is inseparable from the "end" which it is bringing to the world, and, as Albert Schweitzer has so powerfully insisted, the new life of ethical obedience to which Jesus calls his followers is likewise inseparable from the liberation of the believer from the very reality of the world. When the Hellenistic Church once again bestowed upon the world the biblical name of "creation," it thereby abandoned a truly eschatological form of faith. For, in the New Testament, *kosmos* means "old creation." Eschatological faith can never detach the world from its coming end.

Eschatological faith is also dialectical. The Kingdom of God and *kosmos* are antithetical categories. The very dawning of the Kingdom of God places in question the reality of the world; when the Kingdom is fully consummated, the world must disappear. But Hellenistic Christianity assumed a non-dialectical form: the world became the arena of sanctification, redemption now takes place without any effect upon the actual order of the world, and consequently ethics is dissociated from redemption. Adopting the language of Greek ontology, the Church came to know the world as "being" and God as transcendent "Being." The Church thus invested the world with an ontological reality, faith came to know God and the world as existing in a common ontological continuity, and thereby was established what Kierkegaard was to call the great compromise of Christendom. No longer could the Church call for a reversal of the believer's existence in the world, despite the fact that this was the heart of Jesus' message. For Christianity had entered time and history. By transforming its original faith, Christianity had become a "world-affirming" religion. Since that time, Christian theology—at least in its orthodox and dominant forms—has been non-dialectical. Yet now the Christian God is dead! The transcendence of Being has been transformed into the radical immanence of Eternal Recurrence: to exist in our time is to exist in a chaos freed of every semblance of cosmological meaning or order. If the death of God has resurrected an authentic nothingness, then faith can no longer greet the world as the "creation." Once again faith must know the world as "chaos." But, theologically, the world which modern man knows as "chaos" or "nothingness" is homologous with the world that eschatological faith knows as "old aeon" or "old creation"— both worlds are stripped of every fragment of positive meaning and value. Therefore the dissolution of the "being" of the world has made possible the renewal of the stance of eschatological

faith; for an ultimate and final No-saying to the world can dialectically pass into the Yes-saying of eschatological faith.

I V

If Kierkegaard founded modern theology, one is also tempted
to say that Kierkegaard is the only truly modern theologian.
For he is the only theologian whose mode of religious understanding has been consistently dialectical: faith neither enters
into union with the world nor does it stand in isolation from
the world; faith is always the product of a dialectical negation
of the world, of "history," and of "objectivity." Nevertheless,
we must remember that dialectically Kierkegaard's method has
two grave limitations: it never moves beyond the level of negation, and consequently it never reaches the level of the *coincidentia oppositorum*. While a definition of faith as subjectivity
—*i.e.*, authentic human existence culminates in faith—could be
real in Kierkegaard's time, it can no longer be so at a time
when the death of God has become so fully incarnate in the
modern consciousness. Today theology is faced with the overwhelming task of establishing a dialectical synthesis between a
radically profane "subjectivity" (*Existenz*) and an authentically
biblical mode of faith. Obviously this definition of theology's
task is dialectical, and, from this point of view, theology can
only succeed if it employs a fully dialectical method. This means
that theology can reach a true *coincidentia oppositorum* only on
the negative ground of the realization of the radical opposition
between *Existenz* and faith. When *Existenz* and faith are known
as true opposites, then the possibility is established of effecting
an ultimate *coincidentia oppositorum*. But such a coincidence
can arise only on the basis of the most radical negation. To stop
short of the deepest negation is to foreclose the possibility of a
dialectical synthesis. That is why Kierkegaard has prepared the
way for a fully dialectical form of faith.

Theologically, the twentieth century was inaugurated by
theology's reaction against the new estrangement which our
time has brought the Christian faith. One form of this estrangement may be observed in Nietzsche's condemnation of the No-

saying of Christianity. Faith, in our time, appears to be opposed to the very existence and reality of modern man; the reality—or illusion—of faith is wholly other than the reality which we know. Thus, in *The Antichrist*, Nietzsche presented an authentically modern reaction to the Christian God:

> God degenerated into the contradiction of life, instead of being its transfiguration and eternal Yes! God as the declaration of war against life, against nature, against the will to live! God— the formula for every slander against "this world," for every lie about the "beyond!" God—the deification of nothingness, the will to nothingness pronounced holy.

Another and intimately related form of Christianity's new estrangement was posed by the historical discovery of the eschatological "scandal" of New Testament faith. Modern scholarship unveiled a Jesus who is a "stranger and enigma to our time" (Schweitzer's words) because his whole message and ministry were grounded in an expectation of the immediate coming of the end of the world. The Jesus whom we "know" is a deluded Jewish fanatic, his message is wholly eschatological, and hence Jesus and his message are totally irrelevant to our time and situation. Modern man can know faith only as a "scandal"; faith is wholly other than the reality which we most deeply are. Karl Barth met this "scandal," and thus founded crisis theology, by adopting Kierkegaard's dialectical method, a method which led him to posit an antithetical relationship between the Word of God and the word of man. God's Word —God's Yes—can only appear as an ultimate No to sinful, autonomous and "religious man"; for Barth grounded his position in Kierkegaard's infinite qualitative distinction between time and eternity.

In his commentary on Romans and in his book on the resurrection of the dead, Barth succeeded in grasping the eschatological "end" as an existential *Krisis*. For he translated an eschatological symbol pointing to the cosmic end of the world into a human symbol standing for the crisis created by the situation of sinful man encountering the God of righteousness. Following Kierkegaard's existential thesis that truth is "subjectivity," Barth translated the eschatological symbols of biblical faith into symbols reflecting a crisis in human *Existenz*. So it is that eschatological faith became existential intensity, and thus was established the existential school of Protestant dialectical theology. Quite significantly, when Barth later took up the task of constructing a dogmatics which would be in continuity with the historic forms of the Christian faith, he renounced both his earlier discipleship to Kierkegaard and the dialectical method. Quite possibly Barth realized that a dialectical method must negate all human expressions of the meaning of faith—including the creedal and dogmatic statements of the historic Church—while paradoxically affirming the deepest expressions of "subjectivity" or *Existenz*.

The work of the early Barth has been carried on by various followers, the most important of whom are surely Paul Tillich and Rudolf Bultmann, the one engaging in an ontological and the other in a biblical theology. Although in many ways these theologians are dissimilar, they are united by the dialectical goal of correlating modern man's understanding of himself— which they believe culminates in a despair of the human condition—with the answer to this understanding in Jesus as the Word. Both Tillich and Bultmann employ a theology of immanence which apprehends both the human condition and the word of faith apart from the cosmic and transcendent setting of traditional theology. Again, both take as their starting point the eschatological "scandal" of the Christian faith, which as we have seen is a parallel way of formulating Nietzsche's condemnation of the No-saying of Christianity.

v

For the sake of brevity, and despite the complexities of Tillich's system, we shall, for our present purposes, adopt Jacob Taubes' critique of Tillich's theology. Taubes points out that Tillich tries to escape the historical judgment that Christianity has abandoned its biblical and eschatological roots by the daring method of creating an eschatological ontology. Thus Tillich translates the New Testament eschatological symbols of *this* world and the New Being (Old Aeon and New Aeon) into the ontological concepts of "old" and "new" being, "old" and "new" referring to poles of one continuum of being. The concept of "old being" derives from man's experience of estrangement from being, while the concept of "new being" points to the reconciliation of this estrangement in a fulfillment of being. As Taubes says, Tillich "eschatologizes ontology" and "ontologizes eschatology" in the light of man's present situation: "His entire system rotates around the one eschatological problem: man's self-estrangement in his being and his reconciliation in the 'new being.'" Tillich's apologetical method of correlation attempts to relate the ontological *Krisis* of the human condition with the "new being" which is present in Jesus as the Christ. This method entails the assumption of an ontological continuity between our estranged existence as "old being" and the "new being" of Christ (this is the Protestant existentialist version of the Catholic doctrine of *analogia entis,* for which Tillich has been so fiercely criticized by Barth). Consequently, the "new being" of Christ can only be in continuity with our being (contemporary *Existenz*) if it is an immanent reality which is liberated from all ontological transcendence. Taubes makes the telling point that Tillich's "depth" of being—which is reached by the "ultimate concern" of the existing person—is not a transcendent reality lying beyond the world, but is instead the ultimate ground of the being which we now are. This "ground of being" is God or the Unconditioned, who now becomes simply the "depth" underlying *Existenz.* Thus Tillich translates the transcendent Beyond into an immanent "depth" as a means of making the Christian faith meaningful to our time.

If we grant that Tillich's ultimate concern (he defines faith as being ultimately concerned) produces an existential intensity which deepens man's participation in being, his existence in the immediate moment, does it follow that Tillich has followed Nietzsche's "Dionysian" program of transforming the transcendent into the immanent? Taubes believes that he has. Furthermore, Taubes believes that all modern theologies which mediate between faith and *Existenz* involve ". . . the divine in the human dialectic to the point that the divine pole of the correlation loses all supernatural point of reference." However, this judgment must be questioned if only because Tillich's method is not fully dialectical: for Tillich has negated neither the traditional Western ontologies nor the historic forms of Christianity; instead, he has simply correlated an immanentist and mystical form of the traditional ontology which he borrowed from Schelling—it is certainly not Nietzschean, if only because it remains metaphysical—with a modern and only semi-Kierkegaardian form of Protestant "existentialism." Furthermore, Tillich is incapable of true Yes-saying, for he cannot accept an authentically contemporary form of *Existenz,* and he insists that *Existenz* must culminate in anxiety and despair. Again, Tillich refuses to accept an eschatological form of faith; his "eschatological ontology" inverts eschatological faith by establishing a continuum between "old" and "new" being, and his very system demands that the historical Jesus be sacrificed to an "existential" Word. Nor does Tillich's theology of correlation effect a dialectical *coincidentia oppositorum.* For Tillich's method is only partially dialectical; it employs neither radical affirmation nor radical negation, accordingly it must culminate in a non-dialectical synthesis. Yet it is precisely because Tillich's method is not fully dialectical that it reaches neither eschatological faith nor contemporary *Existenz,* despite the fact that this is the apparent goal of Tillich's method, and surely the real goal of all genuinely modern theology.

Bultmann's theology also proceeds out of the two elements of the modern experience of the eclipse of God and the modern "scandal" of the eschatological foundations of the Christian faith. Like Tillich's, the heart of Bultmann's method lies in the translation of eschatological symbols into categories referring only to human existence. Unlike Tillich, Bultmann's concern is to construct a biblical rather than an ontological theology. However, he is only able to formulate a biblical theology by a process of transforming the cosmic and transcendent dimensions of the New Testament message into an existential anthropology (supposedly borrowed from Heidegger's *Sein und Zeit*, but Bultmann's categories are almost a parody of Heidegger's). By following, in large measure, the original theological method of Barth, Bultmann maintains that the most authentic meaning of the primitive Christian eschatological expectation refers not to a cosmic end of the world but rather to a *Krisis* in human existence. Yet Bultmann is first a New Testament scholar, and a great one, and only secondly a theologian; thus he has gone far beyond the early Barth and recognized that an existential interpretation of the New Testament demands a radical transformation of the original meaning of the New Testament. Hence Bultmann originated the method of demythologizing—here paralleling Tillich's method of correlation—as a means of translating ancient "mythical" eschatological symbols into modern existentialist categories. This method is most clearly revealed in his *Theology of the New Testament*, where the translation takes place so subtly that the reader is scarcely aware that it has occurred at all. Bultmann has never formulated his position systematically and it contains much ambiguity (witness the division between left-wing and right-wing Bultmannians). Moreover, he has freely borrowed many of his most important ideas not only from Heidegger but also from Luther, Kierkegaard, Nietzsche and Dilthey; so much so that one wonders whether his position is capable of either a consistent or a systematic expression—and the enormous literature on Bultmann does much to substantiate this suspicion.

A little perspective reveals important parallels between the methods of Tillich and Bultmann. Both methods are in part dialectical, and both attempt to mediate between an "existentialist" form of Protestantism and a contemporary form of *Existenz*. Again, both attempt to translate the biblical form of eschatological faith into a modern form of existential intensity. Thus Bultmann's method of demythologizing reduces the content (*ihr Was*) of the Gospel to the fact (*das Dass*) of the "revelation," a reduction which intends to maximize the existential offense of the Gospel, while eliminating its offense to the modern scientific mind. Thereby, Bultmann, too, sacrifices the historical Jesus to an "existential" Word.

Yet it is of fundamental importance that neither Bultmann nor Tillich is dialectical enough to rise to an acceptance of Nietzsche's vision of Eternal Recurrence. Both believe that human existence apart from "grace" can only culminate in despair, and thus both have developed a fundamentally hostile attitude toward the modern consciousness. Neither Tillich nor Bultmann will follow Kierkegaard in his negation of Christendom, for both are closed to Nietzsche's proclamation of the death of God. Clinging to the vanishing symbols of a now fallen Christendom, they stand on the "knife-edge" between *Angst* and faith. But it is increasingly apparent that the dialectical theologian is standing on thin air, the cloud is lifting, and now we are beginning to see the illusory nature of a stance that would exist "half-way" in the radical immanence of modern man and "half-way" in the transcendence of Christian faith. Finally, neither Tillich's nor Bultmann's method is fully dialectical. We find here neither the radical faith of Kierkegaard nor the radical doubt of Nietzsche. Yet their methods are partially dialectical, and we may hope that their dialectical methods have saved theology from the temptation of the "positivism of revelation" (Bonhoeffer's words) of the Barth of the *Church Dogmatics*. Indeed, the source of the success of Tillich's and Bultmann's work lies in the dialectical method which they both employ. The time has now come for theology to *deepen* and *extend* that method.

VI

If theology must now accept a dialectical vocation, it must learn the full meaning of Yes-saying and No-saying; it must sense the possibility of a Yes which can become a No, and of a No which can become a Yes; in short, it must look forward to a dialectical *coincidentia oppositorum*. Let theology rejoice that faith is once again a "scandal," not simply a moral scandal, an offense to man's pride and righteousness, but, far more deeply, an ontological scandal. For eschatological faith is directed against the deepest reality of what we know as history and the cosmos. Through Nietzsche's vision of Eternal Recurrence we can sense the ecstatic liberation occasioned by the collapse of the transcendence of Being, by the death of God—and we may witness a similar ecstasy in Rilke and Proust; and, from Nietzsche's portrait of Jesus, theology must learn of the power of an eschatological faith that can liberate the contemporary believer from the inescapable reality of history. But liberation must finally be effected by affirmation, for negation alone must pass into Gnosticism. The believer who says no to our historical present, who refuses the existence about and within him, who sets himself against our time and destiny, and yet seeks release in an "eternity" having no relation, or only a negative relation, to our present moment, is succumbing to the Gnostic danger. Consequently, a faith which nostalgically clings to a lost past, a past having no integral relation to our present, cannot escape the charge of Gnosticism; for a total refusal of our destiny can only be grounded in a Gnostic negation of the world. A genuinely dialectical form of faith can never be Gnostic, for it can never dissociate negation and affirmation; hence its negation of "history" must always be grounded in an affirmation of the "present."

We must understand the contemporary crisis in theology as a crisis arising within theology itself. Theology was born out of faith's will to enter history; now theology must die at the hands of a faith that is strong enough to shatter history. If theology is to transcend itself it must negate itself, for theology can be reborn only through the death of Christendom, which finally means the death of the Christian God, the God who is the transcendence of Being. We must have the courage to recognize that it is the Christian God who has enslaved man to the alienation of "being" and to the guilt of "history." Yet now the contemporary Christian can rejoice because the Jesus whom our time has discovered is the proclaimer of a gospel that makes incarnate a Kingdom reversing the order of "history" and placing in question the very reality of "being." Perhaps we are at last prepared to understand the true uniqueness of the Christian Gospel.

The history of religions teaches us that Christianity stands apart from the other higher religions of the world on three grounds: (1) its proclamation of the Incarnation, (2) its world-reversing form of ethics, and (3) the fact that Christianity is the only one of the world religions to have evolved—or, in some decisive sense, to have initiated—a radically profane form of *Existenz*. Christendom imagined that the Incarnation meant a non-dialectical (or partial) union of time and eternity, of flesh and Spirit; thereby it abandoned a world-reversing form of ethics and ushered in the new age of an absolutely autonomous history (profane *Existenz*). What we know as the traditional image of the Incarnation is precisely the means by which Christendom laid the ground for an inevitable willing of the death of God, for this traditional image made possible the sanctification of "time" and "nature," a sanctification finally leading to the transformation of eternity into time. If this process led to the collapse of Christendom, it nevertheless is a product of Christendom, and faith must now face the consequences of a non-dialectical union of time and eternity. Is a form of faith possible that will effect a *dialectical* union between time and eternity, or the sacred and the profane? Already we can see significant parallels between Nietzsche's vision of Eternal Recurrence and Jesus' proclamation of the Kingdom of God. By accepting "Being begins in every Now" as the deepest symbolic expression of contemporary *Existenz*, we can see that modern profane existence knows a form of the Incarnation. Like its New Testament original, the profane form of the Incarnation isolates authentic existence from the presence of "being" and "history," and it does so dialectically. The Yes-saying of Eternal Recurrence dawns only out of the deepest No-saying; only when man has been surpassed will "Being" begin in every "Now." Let us also note that modern *Existenz* has resurrected a world-reversing form of ethics—*e.g.*, in Marx, Freud, Kafka, and in Nietzsche himself. May the Christian greet our *Existenz* as a paradoxical way through which he may pass to eschatological faith? Surely this is the problem that the crisis of theology poses for us today.

T. J. J. A.

April 9, 1965, was the twentieth anniversary of Bonhoeffer's murder. The secular magazines paid more attention to it than the religious, and the slight Bonhoeffer essay here was written at the request of Grandin Conover, literary editor of The Nation, *and thus written for an audience that had no special background information about the current theological influence exercised by Bonhoeffer.*

W. H.

Dietrich Bonhoeffer

There are several Protestant theologies loose in American intellectual life. The one that is foremost in the much publicized ecumenical movement, and that is decisive in the Protestant-Catholic dialogue, is a more or less ossified version of the theology of Karl Barth. Whenever Protestants talk about art or psychoanalysis or literature, it is a good guess that the massive work of Paul Tillich is informing their discussion. When the knotty problems of American arrogance or the contest between ideological and pragmatic foreign policy is being debated, the work of Reinhold Niebuhr is in the immediate background.

But a strong case can be made that the most decisive theological influence on the younger generation of Protestants today is Dietrich Bonhoeffer, who was martyred by the Gestapo on April 9, 1945.

"Martyred" may beg some questions. *Do* Protestants have martyrs? *Can* they have them? What is a martyr? The word was used fairly often about the late Dag Hammarskjöld, not at the time of his death but on the occasion of the publication of *Markings*. Does a martyr have to die in the presence of God to become a martyr? Socrates and Joan of Arc were martyrs, but Jesus, somehow, was not. Why?

Bonhoeffer was a martyr not only because he died making a very sophisticated theological protest against Nazi tyranny but because he met that other condition we seem to require of martyrdom: he let us know what it is like when one gets ready to die. A martyr is not just a religious man who dies for a cause. He is a man—he could be religious or non-religious—who dies for others, and who has had the occasion to communicate somehow the experience of preparing for death. The German resistance movement produced many authentic martyrs in this sense, but no one of them is a contemporary intellectual influence in the way that Bonhoeffer is. He died at the age of thirty-nine, after about two years of imprisonment, just several days before his prison camp was liberated by the Allies, and less than a month before the conclusion of the war in Europe.

Why have the fragmentary works of this young German theologian acted like a delayed time bomb in America and come into their own so recently? Bonhoeffer is not, it should be noted, an important or influential figure in West Germany or Switzerland, the traditional intellectual centers of Protestant theology. (He is important in East Germany and in Czechoslovakia, but not perhaps for the reasons we value him here.) In this country he is communicating to many young Protestants today because his are the only theological words written in the recent past that can help us understand the new era into which we are moving.

What is this new era? It is not the world of the ecumenical movement, or of dialogue with art, or psychoanalysis, or of the politics of sin. It is the world of the radically accelerating pace of secularization, of the increasing unimportance and powerlessness of religion, of the end of special privilege for religious men and religious institutions. It is the world of the new forms of technology, of the mass media, of great danger and great experiment—what Kenneth Boulding calls the post-civilized world.

Bonhoeffer is teaching a few Protestants what it means to say "yes" to the twentieth century and still somehow to stay recognizably Protestant. A look at a few of his seminal ideas will make this clear. The significant works are *Ethics* and, most importantly, his *Letters and Papers from Prison*. This little book is almost certainly in the process of doing for the sixties and seventies what Reinhold Niebuhr's *The Nature and Destiny of Man* did for the forties and fifties. Three central ideas from this book are in the process of becoming part of the general intellectual equipment of a good many younger observers of the American scene, both those with and those without an interest in what is usually called theology.

First, from the prison letters, there is the affirmation of the coming of age of the world. This is related to the rather silly debate about whether or not we are living in a post-Christian world, but it is not the same thing. Bonhoeffer's conviction that the world has moved out of its adolescence and reached an adult phase implied a new interpretation of the intellectual history of the West since the thirteenth century, and demanded a full, ungrudging, affirmative attitude to the secularizing process which began at that time. He writes in the letter of June 8, 1944, that Christians have ordinarily read this story of secularization as tragic or at least as unhappy, and have tried to find some way of urging the worldly West to return to its religious foundations, or to appropriate the wisdom of the East as a guide, or to search for some new theonomy. In any case, Christians have almost always been offended by the self-assurance of the Western secular man.

> Christian apologetics has taken the most varying forms of opposition to this self-assurance. Efforts are made to prove to a world thus come of age that it cannot live without the tutelage of "God." Even though there has been surrender on all secular problems, there still remain the so-called ultimate questions —death, guilt—on which only "God" can furnish an answer, and which are the reason why God and the Church and the pastor are needed.

Bonhoeffer insists that this traditional Christian uneasiness in the presence of confidence, assurance and independence in man is wrong. God is not a working hypothesis; we must learn to live without him, as if he were not there.

> So our coming of age forces us to a true recognition of our situation vis-a-vis God. God is teaching us that we must live as men who can get along very well without him. The God who is with us is the God who forsakes us (Mark 15:34). The God who makes us live in this world without using him as a working hypothesis is the God before whom we are ever standing. Before God and with him we live without God. God allows him-

self to be edged out of the world and onto the cross. God is weak and powerless in the world, and that is exactly the way, the only way, in which he can be with us and help us. (Letter of July 16, 1944.)

It is fairly clear how the meaning of these passages can be put to work in our day. This is, first of all, a rather untypical Christian reading of modern intellectual history. The movement toward secularism, autonomy, away from God, is approved not so that secularists will applaud, but for theological reasons: *i.e.*, dependence and need are not proper descriptions of man's relationship to God. Bonhoeffer invites us to accept the world without God as given and unalterable. If there is to be a God for the modern world, he will not be found by renouncing the world that can do without him.

There is also, in Bonhoeffer's vision of the world come of age, a rejection of religion as salvation either by transmitting the individual to some protected religious realm, or even as protection from something that, without religion, a man might fall into, like despair or self-righteousness. Put more clearly, Bonhoeffer states that in the world come of age, we can no longer be religious, if religion is defined as that system that treats God or the gods as need-fulfillers and problem-solvers.

There are thus no places in the self or the world, Protestants who listen to Bonhoeffer go on to say, where problems emerge that only God can solve. There are problems and needs, to be sure, but the world itself is the source of the solutions, not God. God must not be asked to do what the world is fully capable of doing: offer forgiveness, overcome loneliness, provide a way out of despair, break pride, assuage the fear of death. These are worldly problems for those who live in this world, and the world itself can provide the structures to meet them.

Familiar intellectual worlds are being rejected by Bonhoeffer and by those who are using him as their navigation chart today—Protestant theologies of correlation, for example, where worldly forms of art and knowledge are used to illustrate the incompleteness or brokenness of the world without God. It need hardly be added that the vulgar world of the problem-solving preacher, the pro-God subway ad, and the slick, vulgar world of the clever T.V. commercial for God, are being set aside as well.

Technically, what Bonhoeffer is saying is that in the modern world that can do without God, the idea of the innate religiousness of man, the religious *a priori*, must be rejected. Augustine has sung lyrically and soothingly to many: "restless is our heart until it comes to rest in Thee." Our response today is, maybe some hearts are, and maybe some are not.

The second idea which marks Bonhoeffer's influence and importance is his plea for a non-religious or religionless Christianity. Because the world is grown up and has moved out of its dependency situation, the God of religion, solving otherwise insoluble problems, meeting otherwise unmeetable needs, is impossible and unnecessary. Thus man cannot be said to need God at all; God is not necessary to man. With this affirmation, the substance of whole libraries of Protestant preaching, evangelism, apologetics and Christian education seems a little thin. If man does not need God, if he is not necessary to our lives, how can there be a God for us? Doesn't this lead to a fatal blurring of the line between belief and unbelief? Is it really possible to pull off, without sophistry or deceit, a definition of the Christian as the godless man?

There are some Protestants who are definitely moving in this direction, seriously considering our time as the time of the death of God whose full advent Nietzsche's madman predicted. Others stop short and claim that we may be able to distinguish between using God and enjoying him, between *uti* and *frui*. Thus, we need to seek out the ways in which the unneeded and unnecessary God may be enjoyed.

The plea for a religionless Christianity is thus a plea to give up all claims for the necessity of religion generally. Christianity —as would be true of any religion and any irreligion—is not necessary. It is merely one of the possibilities available to man in a competitive and pluralistic spiritual situation today. Christians are perfectly free to offer their wares to the world come of age, the religionless world. But they have no head starts, ontological or psychological. This in turn implies no clergy deductions, no tax exemption and no preferential treatment of any kind. Finally, when men say "no" to Christianity, it is a real "no," and not a deeply concealed "yes" masked under a protest against false religion. There are those, Bonhoeffer says, who can make it today without God and without despair and guilt. And their success is just as real as the fulfillment of those who live happily and have a God.

We can begin to see what Bonhoeffer is doing and persuading us to do. He is undermining the traditional Christian confidence in language, argument, debate; in short, our assurance that we can persuade an indifferent world that it really needs God. He is forcing us to shift our center of attention from theology, apologetics, criticism of culture, the problem of communication, and even from hermeneutics, to the shape and quality of our lives. He has enabled us to note, in Protestantism, perhaps he has even brought about, the end of theological confidence, and the beginning of a time of confusion, between theology and ethics. The communication of the Christian in our world is likely to be, at least for a time, essentially ethical and nonverbal. Christians themselves, at work in the world of the twentieth century, saying their "yes" to it as vigorously as possible, provide the dynamic evidence for the truth or falsity of their message.

The time when the real vitality of Protestantism was intellectual and centered in the Academy is at an end. The Protestant continues to engage his unbelieving brother, but he is likely to be engaging him by working alongside him. What distinguishes this Christian from his non-Christian comrade? If there is any answer to that, it may well be found by meditating on the third, and most elusively powerful, of Bonhoeffer's ideas, written nine months before he was hanged: "Man is challenged to participate in the sufferings of God at the hands of a godless world." (The letter of July 18, 1944.)

W. H.

From the end of December, 1963, until August, 1964, I was in Chicago on sabbatical leave, devoting most of my time to a study of William Blake, again as a part of my project of seeking a Christian dialectical vision. In the fall of 1964, I completed a manuscript embodying the results of this study, and I was persuaded that I had reached the point where I could begin a new kind of theological inquiry. A splendid opportunity presented itself when Bill Hamilton invited me to give four lectures at the Colgate-Rochester Divinity School. One of these lectures was intended to be a dialogue with Hamilton, and parts of it were inspired by his writing. Later the lecture, in a somewhat abbreviated form, was published under the title of "Word and History" in Theology Today.

While I was writing the above lecture, Dean Stanley Romaine Hopper of the Drew Graduate School called to ask me to give a lecture in their colloquium on dialectic and the sacred. This year the colloquium was being presided over by Owen Barfield. Norman O. Brown had introduced me to Barfield's writings about a year earlier, I was entranced with their power, and had just published a review article on two of his books. I decided to write a lecture that would both strive to meet Barfield's challenge and further my dialogue with Mircea Eliade. Later this lecture was accepted for publication by History of Religions, but was released for this book. I owe a debt of gratitude to an editor of the journal, Charles H. Long, for suggesting a title for this piece—"The Sacred and the Profane: A Dialectical Understanding of Christianity."

T. J. J. A.

Word and History

Theology, as Christians commonly understand it, is seldom conceived to be a unique creation of Christianity. Theology first appears in Western literature in Hesiod's *Theogony*, and appears there as systematic discourse about the acts of divine or sacred beings. It is probable that Hesiod intended to record a peculiarly Greek synthesis of the myths of the Olympian deities with the myths of pre-historic Hellas. When theology later assumed a fully philosophic form in Greece, it became either a purely rational expression of Dionysian myth as in Plato, or a complete abandonment of myth as in Aristotle's identification of theology with the metaphysics of Being. We may not speak of an Oriental theology if only because the Orient knows nothing of God in either the Greek or the Biblical sense. It is significant that only under the impact of Greek theoretical thinking did theology arise in Judaism, Christianity, and Islam. H. A. Wolfson writes that scholastic philosophy, or the coming together of the Biblical tradition and Greek philosophy, was founded by Philo and destroyed by Spinoza. This thesis is highly significant, for to this day Judaism resists the very word "theology." Albert Schweitzer identified Paul as the creator of Christian theology, but as A. von Harnack teaches, Paul's theology was not understood by Christendom until the Reformation if even then. In our own day, the two most important studies of Paul, those of Schweitzer and Rudolf Bultmann, interpret his theology as being either a consistent expression of eschatological mysticism, that is to say as being wholly antithetical to philosophical thinking, or as an understanding of sin and grace that can become fully meaningful only by means of modern existentialism, a philosophy that has set itself against the Western philosophic tradition. We are increasingly coming to understand that the Bible itself can be understood in its own terms only to the extent that it is detached from both the moral and the intellectual categories of Western culture. Yet this must mean that theology can now assume a Biblical ground only by abandoning its own tradition. To become itself, theology must negate itself. Only such a dialectical negation can save the meaning of faith from the darkness brought on by the collapse of Christendom.

The preceding statements illuminate the distinctive nature of Christian theology. Christian theology is neither a mystical nor a rational unveiling of Being. Christian theology *is* a thinking response to the Word that is present upon the horizon of faith, and thus it is neither a systemization of a mythical vision nor a metaphysical or mystical system. The Christian Word appears in neither a primordial nor an eternal form; it is an incarnate Word, a Word that is real only to the extent that it becomes one with human flesh. Archbishop Söderblom has judged the uniqueness of Christianity to lie in the fact that here revelation has the form of "man." No word can be accepted as a Christian Word which appears in an abstract, an inhuman, or a non-historical form. In the words of William Blake: "God only acts and is in existing beings or men." A word must be judged to be non-Christian if it cannot appear and become real in a present and human act of faith, and it is non-Christian to the extent that it cannot become incarnate in the immediate horizon of faith. The judgment is not non-Christian in an absolute or universal sense, but rather non-Christian in the moment at hand, in the actual now to which the Christian Word is directed.

Paul's theology, although it failed to assume a systematic form, revolved about a response to the advent of a New Creation, a New Aeon or New Being that delivers its participant from the Old Aeon of sin, the Law, and the "flesh" (*sarx*, or existence apart from grace). Paul celebrated a New Covenant, a new life of freedom in Christ or the Spirit that annuls the old covenant of Sinai and the Torah of Israel's priestly and legal traditions. Apart from the eschatological situation of the triumph of the New Creation, Paul's theology is simply meaningless. Or, rather, it can be appropriated only in a non-Pauline or non-biblical form, as was done by St. Augustine when he understood Paul's thinking by employing the moral categories of Stoicism and the ontological categories of neo-Platonism. Even Luther was unable to arrive at an eschatological understanding of the Crucifixion and the Resurrection, and thus was forced to introduce a non-eschatological dualism into his thinking. This dualism has plagued Protestant theology throughout its history. One must not, however, condemn the Christian theological tradition for its failure to reach a full biblical form. There must be a recognition that Christian theology can speak only to the historical moment before it. If the primitive Christians alone were participants in a fully biblical moment of faith, then faith in this New Testament form is closed to their Christian descendants. The Christian disciple cannot seek the presence of Christ in a moment of time that is irrevocably past; he must open himself to the Incarnate Word that is present in his own time and space. Faith in Jesus Christ demands a response to a Word that is present in the life of every human hand and face.

There continues to be much to learn from Kierkegaard, a man who not only arrived at a radical and dialectical understanding of faith, but who did so in the context of the advent of a world that is totally profane. Kierkegaard identified faith as "subjectivity," a subjectivity that is the dialectical negation of the "objectivity" that has progressively but decisively evolved in history. The act of faith is a reversal of profane history, a leap across the dead bones of Christendom to contemporaneousness with Christ. When Kierkegaard finally came to believe that the Christianity of the New Testament no longer exists, that contemporary Christianity is exactly the opposite of New Testament Christianity, he reached a consistent fulfillment of his earlier understanding of faith. A truly dialectical leap of faith is inseparable from its ground in an absolutely profane moment of time and space. Just as the apocalyptic New Aeon of primitive Chirstianity appears only in the context of the seeming triumph of the Old Aeon of darkness, a total act of faith in Christ demands a dialectical movement occasioned by the presence of the radical profane. Consequently, faith, in its Christian expression, must repudiate a non-dialectical dualism. Wholly to isolate flesh from Spirit, or light from darkness, or sin from grace, or the sacred from the profane, is to embark upon a path which must inevitably lead to a disintegration of the very act of faith. If a Pascal, a Kierkegaard, or a Dostoevsky never reached a faith that is a haven from darkness, a certainty or a purity that is free of the temptation to despair, then one must recognize that the truest expressions of faith are dialectically united with the very opposite of faith. Likewise the Word of Christianity is inseparable from the concrete actuality of time and space. It was precisely because Kierkegaard was so profoundly open to the spiritual emptiness of his time that he was able to reach a radical understanding of faith. Only on the basis of a full acceptance of the reality of that emptiness was he able to create an existential conception of faith as subjectivity, and thus it was only when he came to realize the death of historical or objective Christianity that Kierkegaard fulfilled his own conception of faith.

More than a century after Kierkegaard, theology has reached the point where it must confess the death of God if it is to survive in the presence of history. Perhaps the greatest theological problem of our time is an understanding of the meaning of the death of God. While it has only been quite recently that the professional theologian has been willing to acknowledge that the Christian God is dead, the disappearance of the historical Jesus from New Testament research clearly testifies to the collapse of the traditional form of faith. It was a Christian and scientific probing into the meaning of the Gospels that led to the dissolution of the historical person of Jesus. True, a Bultmann could follow Kierkegaard and believe that the absence of an objective knowledge of Jesus provides the way to an existential decision of faith. Nevertheless, the fact remains that here the historical Jesus becomes disjoined from the Word of faith, and all too naturally the priestly followers of Bultmann have reinstituted a quest for the historical Jesus as a means of reviving a Protestant form of orthodoxy. When the person of Jesus disappears from the Christian consciousness, the Christian faith seems to lose that very anchor which occasioned its beginning. Yet, Blake believed that ever since the resurrection Jesus has been imprisoned in Vala's Veil—Blake's symbol of the repressive "Mystery" of the Church—and can no longer appear in his original redemptive form. Increasingly there is the recognition that to the extent that we imagine Jesus in his traditional Christian form we are closed to his contemporary presence. The Gospel portraits of Jesus are inseparable from modes of belief and understanding that long since have become impossible for us, whether or not they are products of the Hellenistic community of faith. To cling to these traditional images of Jesus is to pose an insuperable barrier to the appearance of Jesus in our flesh. Jesus can appear neither as an apocalyptic Son of Man nor as an eternal Son of God, nor can we isolate the historical Jesus from the "mythological" categories of the New Testament. Bultmann brilliantly demonstrates that to discard the mythological framework of the New Testament is to negate the historical Jesus, and, as well, to negate both the cultic Christ and the cosmic Logos. Grant as we may the unquestioned power and reality of the Church's image of Jesus, we can scarcely deny that it has disappeared from our history, and with it has disappeared every possibility of mediating the New Testament Jesus to our time and space.

The disappearance of the historical Jesus is but a particular expression of a far deeper reality, the death of God. The theologian must be prepared to recognize that the death of God underlies every mode of our thought and experience. Furthermore, the very ground of Christian theology calls upon the Christian theologian to recognize the death of God as an historical event. Too many Christian theologians have been attracted to Martin Buber's idea of the "eclipse" of God. In *Two Types of Faith,* an exposition of the Jewish and Christian types of Biblical faith, Buber asserts that the Jew can be safe in a time of God's eclipse because he exists in an eternal covenant that cannot be annulled by an act of man. The contemporary Jew can experience the contradiction of our existence as a theophany. However, not existing in an eternal covenant with God—if only because he exists in an Incarnate Word—the Christian cannot know the death of God as a theophany. Nor can the Christian join a Simone Weil in waiting for God. If the Christian is called into an immediate and historical covenant before him, he must fully open himself to the ultimate meaning of his own time and place, and live the reality of his own destiny with the conviction that the Word is to be found here and nowhere else. To wait for another historical destiny, or to speak the name of God in the presence of his absence, is to renounce the very reality of the Incarnation, and to close himself to the presence of Jesus. If God is dead in the life of faith—and this truth is prophetically apparent in the great Christian visionaries of the nineteenth century—then the theologian must fully acknowledge that the Christian God is dead. God is not simply hidden from view, nor is he lurking in the depths of our unconscious or on the boundaries of our infinite space, nor will he appear on the next turn of an historical wheel of fate. Totally committed as he is to the full epiphany of faith in the concrete moment before him, the contemporary Christian must accept the death of God as a final and irrevocable event.

To speak of the death of God as a final and decisive event is to open oneself to the horizon of our history as the full arena of faith. This has not always been the way of Christian faith. It has only been in the course of a long movement of a particular history, the history of Christendom, that Eternity has been swallowed up by time itself, that a radical finitude has appeared which has dissolved the very meaning of transcendence. Earlier Christians could greet the world as the creation, as a contingent realm deriving its ultimate meaning and reality from a transcendent Creator, even though the primitive Christians looked upon the world as the old creation, an Old Aeon that even now is coming to an end. Scholastic philosophy, as Max Scheler teaches, could know finitude as sheer contingency—*i.e.*, as being wholly dependent upon a reality outside it—because medieval Christendom experienced nature as the creation. When an autonomous nature and an infinite space dawned in the Renaissance, the world was no longer manifest as the creation, and with the subsequent triumph of modern science, contingency in the medieval sense has disappeared from view. The world is no longer meaningful by means of anything which might lie beyond it. If a new meaning of nature has pervaded modern history, an autonomous world existing in-itself, then so likewise man himself no longer appears as the image of a transcendent Creator. Increasingly he has become manifest as the product of a series of particular historical and existential situations. Isolated from both the natural and the transcendent realms, the human creature has become its own creator, an autonomous consciousness existing for-itself, despite the fact that in our own time the human consciousness has become a solitary subjectivity progressively dissolving itself. Lament as we may the vanished world of Christendom, it is not present to us, and we must also come to recognize that with the erosion of Christendom we can no longer respond either interiorly or cognitively to the classical forms of Christian belief.

A great many contemporary theologians believe that the new worldliness or the hard secularity of the contemporary world does not touch the interior depths of faith. Indeed, theologians have celebrated the advent of the full worldliness of the world as an occasion for the epiphany of a truer form of faith. Granted that most such statements are naive and unthinking, a dangerous rhetoric underlies many of these joyous announcements. If ours is a world in which the Christian God is dead—and this is the real meaning of theological language which speaks of the triumph of worldliness—then it is an idle and irresponsible fantasy which would imagine that either faith or the Church can survive in their traditional forms. Quite frequently the theologian who rejoices in a new worldliness will reveal that such worldliness simply impels him to an interior and pseudo-historical realm, a world where faith can shine in its original and pristine glory, but also a world that is untouched by the actualities of history and free from the threats of scientific thinking and the assaults of the creative imagination—in short, the world of a simple and unreflective Christian piety. We have only to observe the work of Teilhard de Chardin to grasp the revolutionary consequences for a faith that would engage in a real encounter with our world. It is true that Teilhard occasionally and inconsistently introduces traditional Christian language into the pages of *The Phenomenon of Man;* but this fact scarcely obviates the truth that virtually the whole body of Christian belief either disappears or is transformed in Teilhard's evolutionary vision of the cosmos. Moreover, in *The Divine Milieu*, Teilhard reveals that a religious life which would respond to the death of God cannot direct its prayer or meditation to a transcendent or numinous realm, but instead must open itself to a divine "center" that fills the whole body of the cosmos, and a "center" that has no existence apart from the movement of the cosmos itself. Numerous critics have pronounced *The Divine Milieu* to be the only original Christian treatise on the interior life of prayer to be produced in the twentieth century. If this is true, we can only conclude that even Christian meditation cannot survive in its traditional form in the presence of the death of God.

Confronted as we are by a new and revolutionary moment of history, we can accept our destiny only by acknowledging the loss of all our traditional Christian images. No sacred images whatsoever are present upon our horizon. The original form of Jesus has disappeared from view, transcendence has been swallowed up by immanence, the events of our salvation history have passed into the dead and lifeless moments of an irrevocable past, no heaven can appear above the infinite stretches of a purely exterior spatiality, and no grace can appear within the isolated subjectivity of a momentary consciousness. May we hope that the time has at last arrived when the Christian faith can transcend the language of images? Is the moment at hand when Christianity can fulfill its heritage of a Torah that forbids all images even while giving witness to a total union between the Word and the world? Has the time finally come when Christianity can move beyond even those higher expressions of mysticism which transcend the images and the language of religion? To speak to these questions we must first note the relationship between Christianity and those higher forms of Oriental mysticism which discard all images.

Whether they speak of Brahman-Atman, Purusha, Nirvana, Sunyata, or Tao, the various forms of Oriental mysticism give witness to an eternal and primordial Reality, a passive and quiescent Reality without energy or motion, and a Reality that only truly appears through the disappearance or inactivity of all other reality whatsoever. The Oriental mystic follows a path leading to a dissolution of consciousness, an inactivity of the self, or a total transformation of a spatial and temporal existence into an infinite and eternal Being. These purer expressions of the mystical way are consummated in the epiphany of a primordial Totality, a Totality that reveals itself as being the underlying reality of a seemingly fallen cosmos, and a Totality that is the original source of the polarities of consciousness and the antinomies of history. Yet it is of crucial importance for our purpose to note that the way of the Oriental mystic is a way *backwards*. He must reverse the movements of consciousness and history if he is to unveil the primordial Totality. His goal is the primordial Beginning that existed before the advent of the cosmos or history; the eternal Now which he celebrates is a Now existing prior to the manifestation of time and history.

Simply to speak of Oriental mysticism in the context of a discussion of Christian theology is to open oneself to a realization of the presence of Oriental or non-Christian motifs in the traditional expressions of Christian meditation and belief. If we were to identify a backward movement to a primordial and quiescent Totality as the ground of Oriental mysticism, then we must acknowledge that a Christian doctrine of God as an eternal and impassive Being shares this fundamental ground with Oriental mysticism. So, too, do a Christian nostalgia for a lost paradise, a Christian doctrine of Christ as the eternal

Logos, and a Christian meditation that sinks into the interior depths of the self. Furthermore, when Christianity is seen in this perspective it can only suffer in comparison with Oriental mysticism, for in this form it never reaches the purity, the depth, or the consistency of the Oriental vision. Yet it is precisely by looking for the distinctiveness or the uniqueness of Christianity that the Christian faith can be preserved and enhanced by this challenge. Rudolf Otto in his study of mysticism in East and West, *Mysticism: East and West,* compares Meister Eckhart and Shankara and reaches the conclusion that the distinctiveness of Christian mysticism lies in its celebration of God or the Godhead as a forward-moving process. Whereas Shankara understands Brahman or Sat as existing in an unmoving repose, Eckhart conceives of the Godhead as a life-process, a process whose true reality derives from its very movement. Otto's great study of the eschatological proclamation of Jesus discovers the fundamental and distinctive motif of Jesus' message to lie in its announcement of the "dawning" of the Kingdom of God, a dawning that is itself a forward-moving process, a process whereby a future and transcendent Kingdom penetrates from the future into the present, from its place in the Beyond into this world, and is operative here as an inbreaking realm of salvation. With Otto can one conceive the uniqueness of Christianity to be its affirmation of the sacred or the numinous Reality as a forward-moving process that even now is in process of realizing itself?

This understanding of the ground of Christianity must inevitably lead to a realization of the dynamic and self-transfiguring quality of the Christian Word. Existing neither in a static nor an eternal form, the Christian Word can never wholly or finally be confined within a particular set of images, nor can it perpetually be bound to a particular culture or history. As an active or a forward-moving process it must necessarily negate its particular expressions, and progressively transform itself as it becomes incarnate in a continually changing series of historical moments. At a moment of crisis faith must have an inevitable temptation to return to an earlier or even a primordial form of the Word, but such a path is fundamentally a repetition of the universal mystical quest, and can by no means be judged to be a positive witness to the Word that becomes incarnate in the world. Moreover, priestly religion in all its expressions binds its adherents to a particular Word and a particular community as the sole arena of the redemptive sacred. It isolates and solidifies the events of salvation history into a series of unique and once and for all events. Again, priestly religion, in both its Christian and non-Christian expressions, is a backward-moving remembrance or re-presentation *(anamnesis)* of the sacred events of the past or the primordial Beginning. To employ Kierkegaard's categories in a different context, priestly religion is a "recollection" of all that which has been, and it acts by repeating backwards. But the uniquely Christian form of the Word of faith demands that it express itself in a movement of "repetition," a forward-moving recollection wherein that which has been becomes anew. A Kierkegaardian movement of repetition is impossible for a form of faith that is bound to a sacred history of the past, and so likewise the backward movement of recollection must reverse the forward movement of the Incarnation.

Our situation calls upon us to negate the religious forms of Christendom just as the reform prophets of the Bible called for a new form of faith that negated the pre-exilic forms of Israel's religion. Since the institution of the Church the task of the theologian has primarily been a priestly one. He has been called upon to give meaning to the life of the cult, to reconcile the developing life of the Church with its Biblical ground, to mediate between the Church and the world, and above all to be an apologist for the Church to the world. For the most part the theologian has accepted the sacred history of his particular community as an inviolable given or as the very foundation of theology itself. Yet we must remember that the Biblical prophet spoke against the sacred history of his time. His task was not to link the present and the past but rather to forge a way from the present to the future, and thereby to make possible a new and more radical form of faith. Speaking in the situation of an impending catastrophe to his people, he called them out of their life in an old history of the past and pointed the way to the final moment of the Eschaton. Jesus was such a prophet, but unlike his prophetic forebears he celebrated the immediate dawning of the Eschaton and gave himself to a total negation and reversal of history. By giving himself so fully to the Eschaton of the future, Jesus was, in the words of Schweitzer, crushed by the wheel of destiny, and even the form by which his disciples remembered him has perished in the disintegrating moments of our history. Nevertheless, we know his Word as a Word pointing to an eschatological future, and we must not be dismayed if it is no longer meaningful as a Word of the past. Only by shattering all those images of Jesus that are present in our past can we be open to an eschatological end.

While the Jew awaits a Messiah of the future, the Christian knows that the Messiah-Son of Man has come in Jesus Christ, that his coming was a real and decisive event, and that he will be present with us even to the coming of the end of the world. Despite the fact that we can no longer know him in the images of the Christian tradition, we know that he is present in his Word, and that Word is a Word reconciling the world to itself. But if we are to believe in a real process of reconciliation we cannot believe that the Word itself is unaffected by its act. Nor can we believe that the Word acts through a fleeting series of Gnostic mirages and masks. From the words of Paul, we know that the Word becomes kenotically incarnate in its own Other. It becomes what it beholds, it speaks itself in the speech to which it responds, it acts itself in the joy and pain which it transfigures. In short, the Christian Word is an historical Word. This does not mean that it is a Word which is simply present in a sacred event of the past, nor does it mean that it is merely addressed to historical events, or confined to an historical realm. It means that the Christian Word becomes fully incarnate in the concrete actuality of human flesh, that it is present wherever that which has been becomes anew, or wherever the present seeks fulfillment in a redemptive and eschatological future. Only by a continual process of negating its own past expressions can the Word be a forward-moving process, and only by a process of reversing the totality of history can the Word be an eschatological Word breaking from the future into the present. It is precisely the forward movement of history that testifies to the presence of the Word. Such a movement is a real movement. It is not a perpetual cycle revolving about itself, but a movement opening into the Eschaton of the future, an Eschaton that dawns wherever history negates its past to realize its future. While an eschatological movement of the Word must necessarily negate the past moments of its own expression, it does so not to negate the reality of history itself, but rather to annul a past which forecloses the possibility of a realization of its own future.

Therefore we must recognize that to understand the Christian Word as an historical Word need not mean that it is identified with a history that is past. Historicity is the realm of concrete and actual events, of humanly meaningful events, and when an historical event ceases to exist in a meaningful relation to the present it thereby passes into a non-historical realm. When a contemporary Christian confesses the death of God he is giving witness to the fact that the Christian tradition is no longer meaningful to him, that the Word is not present in its traditional form, and that God has died in the history in which he lives. Insofar as such a Christian is undergoing a full encounter with history he can by no means be judged to be non-Christian, for it is precisely the meditation between faith and history that lies at the center of the Christian faith. Faith has no security against history because history is the arena of faith, and apart from history the Christian reality of faith would perish. It is rather the faith that cannot exist in history that has ceased to be Christian. But it is just for this reason that the contemporary Christian is called to confess the death of God. If God has died in our history then he is no longer present in the Word of faith, and at most he can be no more than a nostalgic memory of an age that is past. At worst he can be a positive barrier to the realization of faith. Buber has said that the modern age is dominated by a Paulinism without grace—we are overwhelmed by alienation, despair and guilt, but we know nothing of Paul's celebration of faith, hope, and love. We might translate these words into our context by saying that the Christian must now know a Paulinism without God. Gradually it is becoming apparent that the *Angst* of modern man is not created by an encounter with an abstract Nothing. It is occasioned by the presence of that nothingness which has followed in the wake of the death of God. Our nostalgia for God has created our *Angst,* just as our demand for an unchanging absolute has hurled us into meaninglessness. Kierkegaard judged *Angst t*o be a product of sin, and when we remember that the late Kierkegaard came to understand sin as the opposite not of virtue but of faith, then we must ask if *Angst* is created by the evasion of history, by faith's refusal to exist in the moment before it. A faith that dares to live in our present will not seek a God that lives in the past. It cannot know an *Angst* that derives from a longing for the God who is the transcendence of Being, and it will be free of a nostalgia for a sacred time that is irrevocably and finally past.

Can we speak of a theology without God? Already in the nineteenth century Blake and Dostoevsky proclaimed a Christ who can be known only by passing through the death of God, and, if we are radical enough, we might understand that Hegel and Nietzsche were Christian thinkers who grasped the necessity of a theological atheism. However, we should not be tempted to think that such a theology knows a God above God or a Godhead lying beyond the God who appears in history or religion. A mystical understanding of the Godhead was no doubt a Christian possibility at a time when God was still present in history. Yet no possibility lies before us of moving from God to the Godhead if only because God is no longer present to us. Even St. John of the Cross's "dark night of the soul" lies intermediate between the presence of God and a total union with the Godhead. The Christian today is called upon to say No to God because God himself has ceased to be present in history. He is present to us only in his absence, and to know the absent or the missing God is to know a void that must be filled with despair and rebellion, an *Angst* deriving from a *ressentiment* that is itself created by an inability to bear a full existence in the present moment. If God has truly died in our history, then he must be negated by the Word of faith. It is the Christian who must murder God, or, rather, it is the Christian who must bury the decomposing God who continues to haunt our memory of things past. A Christian atheism says No to God because of its response to a Word that appears without God; simply to acknowledge that ours is a history in which God is dead is to foreclose the possibility of God's manifestation in the Word. In this situation a Word that appears as the Son of God cannot be a Christian Word, for it is Christ himself who negates every Word that calls its hearer to a primordial or non-historical realm. Finally, as Blake envisioned, it is the human body of Christ who negated the God who is present in the memory of the past, and only when the Christian has wholly been delivered from remembrance and recollection will he be open to the Word that is fully incarnate in the present.

Classical Christian theology knew a tension between time and Eternity, a tension created by the chasm between the creation and the Creator. When the Creator disappears from the boundary of finitude, and Eternity is swallowed up by time, then theology must lose its ground in a dialectical tension between the here and the Beyond. Once, the Church could know Christ as the cosmic Lord, as the Mediator between time and Eternity, as both fully man and fully God. But Christ cannot appear as God at a time in which God is dead. The Christ who appears in the form of a transcendent Lord is inseparable from the actual presence of the transcendent Creator, and with the collapse of the transcendent realm the Word itself can no longer appear in the form of transcendence. Dietrich Bonhoeffer teaches that the presence of Christ can be known only in the body of a broken and suffering humanity, for the Jesus whom we know is wholly detached from the divine attributes of his traditional image. For the first time in its history, theology is now called to a radically kenotic Christology. Already a grave danger besets this new vocation of theology. Our temptation in this situation is to seize upon those New Testament images of Jesus that are seemingly free of a transcendent ground with the hope that we can thereby arrive at an image of a fully contemporary Jesus. Unfortunately, and as New Testament scholarship has long since demonstrated, there are no New Testament images of Jesus that are independent of the theological thinking of the early Church. Thus when we attempt by this means to unveil a fully human Jesus we discover that we are left with the empty shell of a once vital faith. All too naturally the major thrust of contemporary theology has been to dissociate Jesus and the Word, either to apprehend a Word that is wholly isolated from the Church's memory of Jesus or to affirm a Jesus who is liberated from the Word of the Church. In one direction, theology is drawn to an abstract, an inhuman and a non-historical Word, and, in the other, it is drawn to a Jesus who gradually but inevitably collapses into the shrunken humanity of our own time. Is there no way open to us leading to a fully human Jesus or to an authentic Christian Word? Must we continue to wholly identify Jesus with a broken humanity or with an abstract and finally meaningless Word? At bottom these questions impel us to ask if we are in fact living in a post-Christian age, a time in which the Christian Word is silent.

Despite the fact that numerous theologians are now speaking of our time as a post-Christian age we must note that it is impossible for the Christian to dissociate the reality of his own time from the presence of Christ. To speak of an actual or historical time as being isolated from the Word is to speak a non-Christian language. When a Christian speaks of his own time as a time that is not united with Christ he should do so with the confession that he is not speaking the language of faith. Even if we were to adapt a Lutheran language and to speak of the Christian's life in the world as being simultaneously faithful and faithless, we must nevertheless acknowledge that faith in its Christian expression can never be severed from the actual presence of an Incarnate Word. Rather than speaking of our time as a post-Christian age, the contemporary Christian might more truly say that the Word appears in our history in such a way as to negate its previous expressions. It is a particular Christian history, the history of Christendom, that has died in our midst, and it would be nothing less than blasphemy for the Christian to identify the Church with Christendom or to believe that the Word is confined to a history that is past. If the Incarnate Word is a Word that makes all things new then we must not naively believe that it is only the world and not the Word which is affected by the process of Christian "repetition." Such a conception isolates the Word from the world and renounces the reality of the Incarnation. An historical Word is a Word in the process of its own realization and it can move only by negating its own particular expressions. In our situation, a Word that fails to negate its image in Christendom would indeed become motionless and silent. The very fact that Christendom is collapsing about us and within us can be greeted by the Christian as a decisive witness to the contemporary presence of the Word. However, must we not finally define Christendom as all that history existing in the presence of the Christian God? A recognition that the Christian God is a creation of Christian history—of the coming together of Word and history in a particular time and space—can lead to an openness of faith to a new and radical epiphany of the Word in a future beyond the history of Christendom.

Therefore faith must come to know the death of God as an historical event witnessing to the advent of a new form of the Word. As so conceived only the Christian can truly know the death of God because only the Christian is open to the forward movement of history and the Word. Only a new Adam who is liberated from the old creation of the past can celebrate the presence of the Word in a new world that negates all previous forms of faith. After passing through the most abysmal depths of spiritual deprivation, George Bernanos' dying country priest can joyously if feebly announce that everything is grace.

Suffer as we must in a time that has already so ravaged the Christian spirit, we must resist the supreme temptation of despair and renounce every desperate effort to identify a broken and empty humanity as the sole fruit of grace. An eschatological faith knows that grace is *all*, that the Word appears in a new world, a new totality drawing all history into union with the Word. An authentically Christian faith can express itself in No-saying only when confronting a history that is irrevocably past. When meeting the actuality of the history before it, it must give itself to a total Yes-saying, an eschatological repetition of the Word in the present. Since the Christian Word is neither timeless nor primordial, it has no existence apart from its movement. Accordingly, the Christian Word is never silent, nor can it be impassive or speechless. The Incarnate Word speaks in its own movement and nowhere else, and while its movement may well be a process negating its own expressions, it will only cease to be when it ceases to move. The Word that is silent in our time is a Word that has been negated by the Word itself. A faith that clings to the diminishing fragments of a Word that is receding into the past must resist the actual presence of the Word and set itself against the forward movement of the Incarnation. If a new world is dawning in our midst, then the Christian must know this world as an epiphany of the Word, and he must give himself to this new history with the faith that it is precisely at this point that the Word is making all things new. Now that we have reached a point where it is manifest that history itself has moved through the death of God we must celebrate the death of God as an epiphany of the eschatological Christ. While the Christ who lies upon our horizon no longer appears in his traditional form—indeed, he may never again appear in a form that is in continuity with his previous expressions—as Christians we are called into union with his presence among us even when that presence would seem to negate all that faith once knew as the Word. Yet if the Christ of faith is an eschatological Word, he cannot be fully present in the dark and hidden crevices of a turbulent present, nor can he be fully at hand in the broken body of a suffering humanity. He must instead be present in the *fullness* of the history before us. The time is now past when the theologian can be silent in the presence of the moment before him. He must speak to be Christian, and he must speak the Word that is present in our flesh.

T. J. J. A.

The Sacred and the Profane: A Dialectical Understanding of Christianity

The contemporary student of religion is living at a time when not only the reality but also the very meaning of religion threatens to disappear. Innumerable Christian theologians insist, however naively, that Christianity is not a religion, and humanistic scholars seem unable to employ a meaning of religion that can give direction and purpose to their own work. All of us in some sense must share the fruits of a Faustian dissolution of faith, even when our own labors of Sisyphus have seemingly carried us beyond the Western world. We inevitably think and speak under the impact of a peculiarly Western form of absolute world-affirmation.

Students of religion know that the primal forms of religious discourse are by one means or another dialectical, and thus they must inevitably exist in tension with the dominant modes of contemporary thought and experience. All dialectical thinking directs itself to the negation of the Given, of that which happens to appear or to be at hand. In all the various expressions of its multiple forms, dialectical thinking must set itself against the autonomy of that which appears before it, seizing upon the immediate being which is manifest about it as the initial springboard to its own movement of negation. A dialectical movement is, of course, never a movement of simple or sheer negation. Being neither a Gnostic escape from the world nor a romantic flight from history, dialectical thinking moves by means of a negation that is simultaneously affirmation. The Given is negated only to be affirmed in a transfigured form. Dialectical thinking thinks both to and from what the Western rational mind knows as "contradiction." It appears when a seemingly unbridgeable chasm arises between the True or the Real and the immediately Given, and it culminates in a *coincidentia oppositorum,* a final coming together of those opposites whose initial opposition or contradiction occasioned its own creation. Consequently, dialectical thinking is inseparable from the Given which it must oppose; and it can only appear in conjunction with the manifestation of a Given which itself contains the seeds of its own negation.

Hegel, who identified philosophy with dialectical thinking, also believed that philosophy is identical with religion insofar as both must negate the Given: "For religion equally with philosophy refuses to recognize in finitude a veritable being, or something ultimate and absolute, or non-posited, uncreated, and eternal" (*Logic,* Vol. I, Bk. I, Ch. 3). All expressions of religion must in some sense share such a movement of negation, for religion must necessarily direct itself against a selfhood, a history, or a cosmos that exists immediately and autonomously as its own creation or ground. So it is that critical definitions of religion in all their variety show that the sacred and the religious life is the *opposite* of the profane and the secular life. Just as the prophet calls upon his hearer to turn away from his immediate existence in the world, the mystic envisions an eternal Now that dissolves the time of duration. Furthermore, and as the work of Mircea Eliade has so fully demonstrated, mythical and ritual patterns the world over are intended to effect a negation of concrete time and space leading to a repetition of the primordial Beginning or to a passage to the "Center" of the world. Yet a primordial Beginning and a sacred "Center" are meaningful only insofar as a chasm lies between the sacred and the profane. A profane worldliness is not simply the mask or the veil of the sacred. Only the religious vision can know the world as *maya* or "Old Aeon." Profane worldliness is rather a positive and even absolute defiance or reversal of a sacred existence. In contrast, an existence embodying or pointing to the sacred is the dialectical opposite of existence in the profane. Seen in this perspective, religion itself can only appear or arise in conjunction with a rupture between the sacred and the profane, a rupture testifying to the alienation of immediate existence from a sacred or transcendent ground. Christianity has named this rupture the "Fall," and no religion has so profoundly emphasized the gulf between the sacred and the profane as Christianity. All religions, however, in one way or another witness to the loss of innocence or paradise, just as all religions proclaim or celebrate a way *to* the sacred *from* the profane.

If religion arises as a positive response to the appearance of the world or human existence in a fallen form, then one might expect the movement of religion to revolve about the repetition or re-presentation (*anamnesis*) of a primordial paradise. Conceived in this sense, the idea of an original or primordial paradise is bound to no particular symbolic form, and it could just as readily lend itself to apocalyptic symbols of the End when these are apprehended under the form of a final repetition of a primordial Beginning. It is a striking fact that images of paradise throughout the history of religions bear the marks of a dialectical negation or reversal. Paradise appears in the religious consciousness as a dialectical inversion of the *here* and *now* of profane experience, whether symbolized in a spatial form as celestial transcendence or in a temporal form as the Beginning or the End. An unfallen Beginning can express itself in symbolic form only to the extent that it is known as the opposite of a fallen present. But whether by way of myth and ritual, or through interior meditation or prophetic faith, religion seeks to annul all opposition between the sacred and the profane, thereby seeking a renewal of paradise in the present moment. Both the mystic, who directs himself to the negation or the emptying of consciousness, and the prophet, who calls for a total reversal of all worldly conditions, have chosen a path of abolishing the profane. Yet the sacred that becomes manifest through a negation of the profane must be a primordial Reality, an original paradise that has been hidden or lost by the advent of the profane, and thus a paradise that can be actualized by an unveiling or a reversal of the present. As Proust so aptly remarked, the only true paradise is always the paradise we have lost.

Religion is a quest for the primordial Beginning, a backward movement to an original paradise or a sacred "Center." With its goal of arriving at the primordial Totality, it follows a path of involution, a path that inverts or reverses the evolution of history and the cosmos out of an original Unity, thereby annulling those antinomies which have created an alienated and estranged existence. At first glance it would seem that those higher expressions of religion which proclaim the triumphant realization of the Kingdom of God, or the sole reality of Brahman-Atman, or the blissful totality of grace or Nirvana, do not fall under such a conception of religion since they transcend a tension or opposition between the sacred and the profane. Rather than conceding that the higher expressions of religion transcend the form and the imagery of religion itself, it would be wiser to note that such expressions of religion are fufillments of a universal religious goal. When faith celebrates the final victory of the Kingdom of God, or contemplation becomes totally absorbed in Brahman-Atman or Purusha, or *satori* releases the all-pervading reality of Sunyata or Tao, the profane reality has been totally abolished or annulled. If a Zen practitioner were to say that nothing happens in *satori,* or that truly and actually there is no fallenness, no guilt, no alienation, and no estrangement, then we could only reply that from the point of view of the profane consciousness he has succeeded in abolishing the very memory of the profane. Moreover, if a Zennist were to persist in his denial and to assert that Nirvana is Samsara and Samsara is Nirvana—or that there is no difference whatsoever between the sacred and the profane—we would be forced to respond that his language is only meaningful in the context of the complete dissolution of the profane consciousness. A Buddhism that identifies Nirvana and Samsara can do so only on the basis of a discovery that all existing reality is empty or void *(sunya)* of reality itself, and this discovery is inseparable from an absolute and final negation of a profane reality. This negation annuls the opposition between the sacred and the profane by abolishing both the reality and the memory of the profane opposite itself. On the other hand, if a Christian were to insist that Christianity affirms both the reality and the goodness of the creation, he should simply be informed that originally Christianity was an apocalyptic faith looking forward to the end of the world as the cataclysmic destruction of the "Old Aeon" or old creation, and such an apocalyptic negation of the world is inseparable from a total affirmation of the Kingdom of God. A faith that could look forward to God's becoming all in all could rejoice in the imminent collapse of the reality of the world, thereby celebrating an End that is a repetition of a primordial Beginning. An End that abolishes the creation repeats or re-presents the Beginning that existed *prior* to the creation. Again, a total epiphany of the sacred occurs only by means of a total abolition of the profane.

The forms of Oriental mysticism and Biblical eschatology coincide insofar as they must culminate in an absolute negation of the Given. Only a mystical dissolution or an apocalyptic reversal of the reality of the profane can make possible a final or a total manifestation of the sacred. Even the language by which we speak of the higher expressions of religion is inevitably dialectical. We speak of a mystical *dis*solution or an apocalyptic *re*versal, thereby testifying to the negative movement of religion. Of course, this negation is dialectical. This means that here negation and reversal are grounded in affirmation; time and space are negated in their profane or fallen form only to be regenerated or resurrected in their sacred or primordial form. Underlying all forms of religion is a dialectical movement of repetition; the negation of the immediately Given is but the hither or apparent side of the repetition of the primordial or eternally Given. Negation and repetition are but two sides of the same movement, two manifestations of a single dialectical process, whose meaning or appearance varies solely in accordance with the intention from which it is viewed. From the perspective of the immediately or apparently Given, religion is a movement of negation. Yet so likewise from the perspective of faith or vision, religion is a movement of repetition or regeneration. Its seeming negation of the profane is at bottom an epiphany or renewal of an original and primordial sacred. A dialectical negation of time and space culminates in a regeneration of Eternity—a renewal or repetition of a primordial Totality—and therefore an absolute negation of the profane is equivalent to a total affirmation of the sacred. Accordingly, the higher expressions of religion are consummations of the religious movement itself—"Old Aeon" passes into "New Aeon," Samsara is identical with Nirvana. The *coincidentia oppositorum* is a universal religious symbol, a symbol unveiling both the goal and the ground of religion.

All too naturally we employ a Latin phrase in speaking of the "coincidence of the opposites," for it is not too clear if we are speaking of a coincidence, a harmony, a unity, or an identity of the opposites, and with this ambiguity the meaning of the opposites themselves is obscured. When the negative movement of religion is understood as being a *reversal* of the profane, there is a clear implication that religion acts by way of a backward movement or *return*, with the inevitable corollary that the sacred is an original or primordial Reality. Certainly the higher Oriental symbols of the sacred point to an eternal, an inactive, or a quiescent Totality, and a Totality that only truly appears through the disappearance or inactivity of all motion and process. Moreover, it is the very *dis*appearance or *in*activity that repeats or resurrects an original Totality. Here, repetition and resurrection are expressions of a cosmic and universal process of regeneration. Such a process of regeneration, however, is in no way to be identified with a process in space and time. On the contrary, a fully mystical regeneration annuls or dissolves both spatial location and temporal duration; hence, the Oriental mystic invariably speaks of a timeless Eternity, a Nothing, or a Void. Whether by way of the *wu wei* or inaction of Taoism and Zen, or the Yogic discipline of emptying the contents of consciousness, or the purposeless action of the *Bhagavad Gita,* the way of Oriental religions is a way *backwards.* A primordial Totality can be reached only by a reversal of the movements of consciousness and history, and this reversal of the profane is equivalent to an epiphany or renewal of an original sacred. Yet a reversal in this sense can only mean that a profane time and space cease to exist in their own form and movement. Or, rather, a repetition of a primordial sacred reveals the sacred identity of the profane. A mystical regeneration inverts the concrete expressions of time and space, leading to the resurrection of a primordial Totality. A Totality, however, comprehends all reality whatsoever, and a sacred Totality must annul the possibility of profane existence. A *coincidentia oppositorum* in this sense must identify the opposites by abolishing their opposition, an abolition effected by an absolute negation of the profane. *Coincidentia* here must finally mean a non-dialectical "identity," for it is an identity that only appears with the disappearance of the opposites. A mystical epiphany of the primordial Totality dissolves the opposition between the sacred and the profane by annulling the fallen reality of space and time. Space and time then become manifest in their primordial or eternal form, and such an original Totality is free of the polar or dialectical meaning of either the sacred or the profane. Thus the *coincidentia oppositorum* in Oriental mysticism is an identity of the opposites. The profane reality ceases to move or disappears, thereby becoming identical with the sacred, and the sacred now ceases to exist in opposition to the profane.

May we say that the goal and ground of Biblical eschatology is a *coincidentia oppositorum* that likewise identifies the sacred and the profane? Does the prophetic faith of the Bible revolve about a return (or "turning," *metanoia*) to a primordial Beginning? Or does it culminate in an apocalyptic End which is a final repetition of the Beginning? If so, it would seem to follow that an eschatological faith must seek to abolish the opposites either by collapsing the profane into the sacred or by annihilating the form and movement of the profane. Yet such a formulation does violence both to an eschatological faith's engagement with the world and to the New Testament and Christian meaning of Incarnation. Ever since its establishment in the second century, Christian theology has either chosen the language of a purely rational and non-dialectical thinking, or it has repudiated all thinking that is directed to the meaning of its Biblical foundation. In either case, Christian theology has refused a thinking that incorporates the primal forms of Biblical faith, just as it has turned aside from any attempt to think through to its own ultimate implications. Consequently, Christian theology has never sought to unveil the meaning of an apocalyptic *coincidentia oppositorum*. It need not surprise us that such a form of theology has always been uncertain about its religious ground. While frequently claiming that the soul is naturally Christian, or dogmatically if uncritically insisting that Christianity is the fulfillment of the world's religions, Christian theology has nevertheless condemned "idolatry" and opposed all paganism (*i.e.*, non-Biblical religion). The contemporary theologian is even embarked upon a quest for a "religionless" Christianity. Kierkegaard—who conceived of paganism as an immediate relationship to God—already sensed that the Christian faith is grounded in a negation of religion. Unfortunately, neither Kierkegaard nor his twentieth-century followers succeeded in creating a fully dialectical theology. Never being able to break from their Lutheran roots, they have clung to a non-dialectical dualism, and have employed dialectical thinking only to attack the profane expressions of faith. Inevitably such a dialectical theology falls back upon a dogmatic and non-dialectical form of faith or belief, thereby foreclosing the possibility of reaching a *coincidentia oppositorum*. But if Christian theology has the legitimate goal of unravelling the meaning of a "religionless" Christianity, it must take far more seriously than ever before the relationship between Christianity and religion, and this must mean that it is now called to a full encounter with the higher expressions of religion.

Earlier we remarked that Christianity emphasizes the Fall more radically than any other form of religion. The Fall is an actual and real event; the world and human existence are judged to be actually and truly estranged from their original divine ground, and consequently the process of redemption must occur in the arena of concrete time and space. The Fall is never an ultimately real event in Oriental religion. Thus for Shankara it can only be through a great cosmic ignorance or *maya* that God and the world can be known as moving and existing out of the depths of Brahman-Atman; and for Nagarjuna, Nirvana is non-ceasing and unachieved, because there has been no initial Fall, and there is no need for a re-transformation. When the profane is understood as the opposite of the sacred in a wholly negative sense, then the movement of religion must be conceived as an eternal repetition of an unfallen sacred, and the profane reality must be judged to be an illusory mask or veil of the sacred. Only an acceptance or an affirmation of the fallen *reality* of the profane can make possible a faith that encounters the concrete actuality of the world, and moves *forward* through alienation and estrangement to an eschatological End that transcends a primordial Beginning. Just as Christianity is the only religion to have abandoned an original paradise, so Christianity alone among the world's religions affirms the ultimate reality of the Fall, and opens itself to the actual processes of time and space as the arena of redemption. Owen Barfield's distinction between an "original" and a "final" participation—in his fascinating and deeply illuminating book, *Saving the Appearances*—does much to unveil the uniqueness of the Christian faith. Images of paradise invariably testify to a longing or a nostalgia for an original paradise, *i.e.*, for participation in an original cosmic Totality, a Totality present in a primordial time prior to the advent of the rupture between the sacred and the profane, a time when suffering, death, and alienation had not yet come into existence. Barfield identifies original participation as paganism, and insists that the Old Testament's condemnation of idolatry was a negation of original participation. From this point of view, only the loss of original participation or a primordial paradise can make possible a final participation, *i.e.*, an ultimate participation that is reached by moving *through* fallenness and death to a definitive and final reconciliation between the sacred and the profane.

Whether we conceive of religion as a quest for original participation, or as a repetition of an unfallen Beginning which abolishes the opposites by negating the reality of the profane, it is clear that Christianity cannot be judged in this sense to be a religion, or at the very least that the Christian faith is finally directed to a non-religious goal. Insofar as faith in its Christian expression moves through the factuality of estrangement and death, it can never accept a mere negation of the profane. Nor for that matter can a faith accepting the reality of the Fall seek an unfallen sacred or a primordial moment of time. Only an actual reversal of a fallen and profane *reality* can lead to a final participation that transcends a primordial Beginning. Such a reversal would be consistently and radically dialectical. It would occur by means of what Hegel terms "pure negativity" or the "negation of negation," and it would move through the reality of the profane to a final or eschatological sacred that reconciles the profane with itself. Despite the fact that Buddhist logic is grounded in negation, Th. Stcherbatsky, in his magisterial study of Buddhist logic, points out that Indian logic has never known the negation of negation. Only an acceptance of the reality of a negative or fallen reality can make possible a *coincidentia oppositorum* that is a coming together of the dual reality of the sacred and the profane. It is precisely this *coincidentia* of the opposing realms of the sacred and the profane that makes possible Christianity's celebration of the Incarnation as an actual and real event, an event that has occurred and does occur in concrete time and space, and an event effecting a real transformation of the world. Faith, in this consistently dialectical sense, must oppose or negate a sacred that is an unmoving Eternity or a quiescent Totality. A sacred that annuls or transcends the reality of the profane can never become incarnate in a fallen form, and thus it could never affect or transform the given or immediate reality of a fallen world. Only a sacred that negates its own unfallen or primordial form can become incarnate in the reality of the profane. To the extent that faith or vision knows an eternal and unmoving sacred it can never know the reality of the Incarnation.

When religion is conceived as a dialectical movement that culminates in an abolition of the opposites, *i.e.*, as a return to an unfallen and primordial Beginning, then its movement may be understood by means of Kierkegaard's category of "recollection." Believing that recollection is the pagan life-view, a life-view affirming that all that is has been, Kierkegaard conceived of recollection as a backward repetition. From this point of view, all priestly or cultic religion, including its Biblical and Christian expressions, is a recollection or re-presentation (*anamnesis*) of a sacred history of the past. Mystical religion could then be understod as an interior movement of recollection, or as a translation into interior meditation of a cultic and mythical regeneration of history and the cosmos. In either case, religion is a backward movement to an archaic, or sacred, or a timeless past, *i.e.*, a past having only a negative relation to the concrete actuality of the present. But Kierkegaard opposed "repetition" to "recollection," attempting to define repetition as a transcendent or religious movement by virtue of the absurd, while noting that "eternity is the true repetition" (*Repetition*, p. xxii). Repetition, in this sense, must be conceived as a forward movement. Whereas the backward movement of recollection arises from the judgment that all that truly is has been, the movement of repetition embodies the present and actual becoming of an existence which has been. Nevertheless, repetition and recollection are the same movement, only in opposite directions; "for what is recollected has been, is repeated backwards, whereas repetition properly so called is recollected forwards" (*Ibid.*, p. 4). It cannot be said that Kierkegaard thought through the full meaning of his own category of repetition, but it is clear that he intended repetition to have a specifically or uniquely Christian meaning, and that it is the forward movement of Christianity which distinguishes it from its pagan or religious counterparts. Yet such a forward movement cannot culminate in an abolition of the opposites by returning to a primordial Beginning. Like its analogue in the prophetic faith of the Old Testament, it must be grounded in an eschatological End, and it can be consummated in that future End only by moving through a rebirth or renewal of *all* that existence which has been.

Therefore a renewal occurring through a specifically Christian movement of repetition could only culminate in a transformation of the opposites. The opposites cannot be simply annulled or negated, for then there would be neither a forward movement nor an eschatological End. It is precisely because the totality of existence is being re*new*ed or transformed that the opposites cannot be abolished or dissolved. A pagan or religious "recollection" must, it is true, dissolve the opposition between the sacred and the profane, but recollection cannot move forward to eternity. Only a movement through the fallen reality of the opposites can issue in a genuinely New Creation or New Aeon. Conceived in this sense, an eschatological End cannot be a repetition of a primordial Beginning. If Christian repetition makes all things new, then it must abolish or negate a memory or recollection of an original participation, and thus it must negate the movement of negation in religion. With this negation of negation, an original sacred must itself be negated. By this radical negation every image and every expression of the religious movement of recollection must be transcended. Of course, the higher expressions of mysticism have always known a transcendence of images, but they transcend imagery by abolishing the profane consciousness, or by dissolving all that history lying between the present and the Beginning. As opposed to this backward movement of the religious expressions of mysticism, a Christian repetition must move forward beyond the death of a primordial or original sacred to an eschatological *coincidentia oppositorum* that reconciles and unites the sacred and the profane. Quite naturally Christian theology has turned aside from the problem of the meaning of such a movement of repetition, just as it has refused the task of thinking through to its own ground in an eschatological End. Insofar as Christian theology is bound to an eternal and primordial God, it cannot be open to a negation of original participation, nor can it accept the possibility of an End that transcends the Beginning. Nonetheless the most radical Christian seers—who are fully exemplified in their own respective ways by a Blake and a Hegel—have long insisted that it is the Christian God and the Christian religion which are the deepest obstacles to an eschatological, a consistently dialectical, or a total redemption.

The non-dialectical ground of historical Christianity has been unveiled simply by taking up the problem of the dialectical meaning of religion. For not only do the priestly and institutional forms of Christianity submit to the heteronomous authority of a series of events that are irrevocably past, but the thought of the Christian theologian himself has been closed to a truly dialectical meaning of the sacred. None of the schools of Christian theology has been able to accept a fully kenotic meaning of the Incarnation, despite the fact that such a meaning has again and again been declared to be the goal of Christian thinking. If the Incarnation is the descent of God into human flesh, *i.e.*, if Christ in being born in the likeness of men emptied himself of the form of God (Phil. 2:5-7), then a dialectical understanding of the Incarnation must go beyond the New Testament and recognize that a kenotic Christ cannot be known as an exalted Lord or cosmic Logos. Only a theology which abandons an original and primordial sacred, and opens itself to a forward moving process of repetition, can acknowledge that God has truly and actually become incarnate in concrete space and time. When the Incarnation is understood as a descent into the concrete, or as a movement from a primordial and unfallen sacred to an actually fallen profane, then it cannot be conceived as not affecting a supposedly eternal Godhead, or as being a static or unchanging extension of the God who is the transcendence of Being. Nor for that matter can an understanding of the Incarnation as a process of repetition allow the Incarnation to be confined to a once and for all event of the past. A theology which remains bound to the language and imagery of the New Testament must refuse the very thesis that the Incarnation is a forward movement or process. An authentically kenotic movement of "incarnation" must be a continual process of Spirit becoming flesh, of Eternity becoming time, or of the sacred becoming profane. Yet its forward movement is inseparable from a continual process of self-negation or self estrangement. Spirit can continue to become flesh only by negating its own past expressions. A Spirit that ceases to move or to negate itself is no longer an Incarnate Word. Christianity invariably becomes religious at precisely those points where it refuses to become incarnate.

Seen in this perspective, historical Christianity must be judged to be a discordant synthesis between a religious movement of recollection and an eschatological or non-religious movement of repetition. Religious Christianity parallels the non-Christian expressions of religion insofar as it is a recollection of an original or primordial sacred. Here is found a nostalgia for a lost paradise, a re-presentation of a sacred history of the past, and a belief in God as the "Unmoved Mover" who is the pure actuality *(energeia)* of Being. When the Christian God appears as the Wholly Other, the sovereign and transcendent Creator, he is manifest in his *religious* form as a primordial Deity, the El Shaddai of the Book of Job whose very sacrality annuls or negates the existence of the profane. So likewise a Christian faith that lets "God be God" is a submission to a primordial sacred, a recollection of the Beginning, and therefore it cannot respond to an Incarnation which is a movement of the sacred into the profane. Insofar as Christian theology has understood the Incarnate Word as an epiphany of the primordial Deity, it has set itself against the actual process of the Incarnation by understanding it as a backward movement to the Beginning rather than as a forward movement to the End. Only a Word that negates its ground in the primordial sacred can actually *move* into the fallen reality of the profane. To the extent that the Christian Word fails to negate its original form, it cannot be a forward moving process, nor can it be a process of renewal, or a progressive descent into the concrete. Not only does a religious understanding of the Word reverse the forward movement of the Incarnation, but it encloses the Word in a static and lifeless form, thereby isolating its power and confining its role to one of passive quiescence. When the Word is understood as a dynamic movement of Spirit into flesh, then it must be conceived as a process of reversing the original identity of Spirit, and, in contrast, of transforming the fallen reality of flesh. Consequently, a forward movement of repetition must culminate in an abolition of its original ground. The primordial God of the Beginning must die to make possible a union of Spirit with flesh.

"God is dead" are words that may only truly be spoken by the Christian, not by the religious Christian who is bound to an eternal and unmoving Word, but by the radical Christian who speaks in response to an Incarnate Word that empties itself of Spirit so as to appear and exist as flesh. A kenotic Word acts or moves by *reversing* the forms of flesh and Spirit. Moreover, a dialectical reversal in this sense cannot lead to an identification of the sacred with the profane or of the Spirit with flesh; Spirit must negate itself as Spirit before it can become manifest as flesh. When the world is affirmed as an actually fallen and profane reality, then it cannot be known as a mask or veil of the sacred, and the sacred and profane must exist in a state of opposition to each other insofar as each retains its original or primal reality. Such a state of opposition can only be effected by a dual movement of the opposites into their respective Others—Spirit empties itself of Spirit so as to become flesh, and flesh negates itself as flesh so as to become Spirit. True, a forward moving process of repetition culminates in a *coincidentia oppositorum.* Yet *coincidentia* now bears an eschatological meaning. Only at the End will flesh and Spirit become identical, and their identity will be established only when flesh has actually ceased to be flesh and Spirit has perished as Spirit. Thus there can be no question of a fully eschatological *coincidentia* being known as a recollection or an epiphany of a primordial Beginning. Both recollection and repetition culminate in a *coincidentia oppositorum,* but whereas recollection is a backward movement to the Beginning, repetition is a forward movement to the End.

Is Kierkegaard correct in identifying recollection and repetition as the same movement, in opposite directions? Or does a single dialectical movement assume a different meaning and reality in accordance with the direction in which it moves? Just as recollection revolves about an absolute negation of the profane, may one say that repetition revolves about an absolute negation of the sacred? Insofar as the religious movement of negation is dialectical, its negation of the profane is at bottom an affirmation of the sacred. Is it likewise true that a Christian or consistently eschatological negation of an original sacred must culminate in an affirmation of the radical profane? Here, it is true, there is a genuine and actual movement of the sacred into the profane. But does the actuality of this movement derive from the renewal or repetition of the profane? We have seen that a religious repetition of a primordial Beginning annuls or reverses the life and movement of the profane. Can one now say that the process of the Incarnation annuls and reverses an original quiescent Totality, thereby making possible a progressively forward movement and expression of the profane? Simply to raise these questions in the context of our time and situation is to recognize the possibility that the death of God—*i.e.*, the dissolution of all images and symbols of an original sacred, and the collapse of a sacred or transcendent realm underlying this dissolution—is a culminating expression of the forward movement of the Incarnation. When the sacred and the profane are understood as dialectical opposites whose mutual negation culminates in a transition or metamorphosis of each into its respective Other, then it must appear that a Christian and eschatological *coincidentia oppositorum* in this sense is finally a coming together or dialectical union of an original sacred and the radical profane. By a kenotic negation of its primordial reality, the sacred becomes incarnate in the profane. Yet this movement of the sacred into the profane is inseparable from a parallel movement of the profane into the sacred. Indeed, the very movement of repetition and renewal—precisely because it is an actual and concrete movement—testifies to the ever more fully dawning power of the reality of the profane. Consequently, a consistently Christian dialectical understanding of the sacred must finally look forward to the resurrection of the profane in a transfigured and thus finally sacred form.

T. J. J. A.

One of the motifs of the radical theology is its interest in the move from pessimism to optimism in American culture today. This essay suggests how some of the relevant material may be laid out and how some theological responses may be developed, but it is clearly without any satisfactory methodological tools for connecting the optimism with the theological position. "Optimism" is not a wholly satisfactory term, for it suggests naivete and insensitivity to tragedy. What it really means in this context is a willingness to count on the future and a belief in its real improvement.

W. H.

The New Optimism—
from Prufrock to Ringo

Theologies change for many reasons. Old theologies break down, or just lose their effectiveness. Everybody knows, or at least feels, that the time of troubles for the neo-orthodox-ecumenical-biblical-kerygmatic theology has arrived. This theology, once the prophetic disturber of peace, has now become the establishment, and under attack has turned querulous and defensive.

The theological reasons for the deterioration of neo-orthodoxy are beginning to become clear. Neo-orthodoxy was a striking protest against the liberal confidence that God could be possessed, and its return to the dialectic of the presence and the absence of God testified to the way believers felt during the years before and after World War II. The reason neo-orthodoxy is not working today surely has something to do with the collapse of this dialectic, a collapse which is the overcoming of the presence of God by the absence that men are calling the death of God.

There are some non-theological factors in the new theological mood in Protestantism. The most striking aspect of neo-orthodoxy, in America at any rate, was its doctrine of man. *Moral Man and Immoral Society* was a book from the Depression and Reinhold Niebuhr's Gifford lectures were being delivered in Edinburgh as Europe stumbled toward war. Just as we were learning despair and tragedy from daily events, the theological equipment was there to help us interpret what was happening. Neo-orthodoxy was in part a pessimistic theology, even though many have made that point insensitively. As neo-orthodoxy moved into the 1950's taking psychotheraphy, existentialism, I and Thou in its stride, it more and more turned man to his inner world, leaving behind the outer world of politics which gave it its birth in the 1930's and 1940's. It is ironical that neo-orthodoxy, born as a radical protest against liberal conformism, became one of the fashionable ideologies for the Eisenhower period in American intellectual life—that time when men sagely advised us that the real battle was not bohemia or radical politics or ideology, but the mystery of the inner life. Old Niebuhrians tended to go to the back pages of the *National Review* to die. Inner submission, prudent realism, accepting with maturity the tragic structures—all of these styles of the fifties were as readily being justified by neo-orthodox theology as by anti-communism or psychoanalysis.

During this time Hawthorne and Melville were being re-read. Men stopped crying out against injustice and learned to delight in life's complexity and richness, perhaps with Henry James, perhaps with the *Playboy* ads. It was discovered that the tragic sense of life went along quite well with good manners, nice clothes, sensitivity to interpersonal relations, and a good conscience about the rat-race. When Niebuhr, in his famous prayer, distinguished between the things we could change and the things we couldn't, there were—for him—a lot of the first and very few of the second. But by the time the bad gray-flannel-suit novels started and everybody began to talk about conformity, the courage to accept the unchangeable was much more highly prized than the will to change, mainly because in the fifties nobody (besides Rosa Parks and a few others) thought there was much that could be changed. Neo-orthodox theology —though not it alone—created men skilled in avoiding unprofitable commitments, careful about risks, very wise in seeing how not to make fools of themselves. Thanks to it, men became quite at home in this world. These were canny, realistic believers whose wry view of self and others could be as well confirmed by the poet, the existentialist novel, or one's own analyst, as by theology.

I suspect that one of the reasons neo-orthodoxy now doesn't work is that this pessimism doesn't persuade any more.

I have no way of knowing how changes in sensibility come, or how they are identified and tested. But I think optimism is a possibility for many and a necessity for some today in a way that has not been the case in America for some time. Things would, of course, be much easier if one could do without words such as "optimism" and "pessimism." Part of what I mean by the first is an increased sense of the possibilities of human action, human happiness, human decency, in this life.

If one had to choose a date for this change of sensibility, one might, for the fun of it, pick January 4, 1965. On this day, T. S. Eliot died in London, and Lyndon Johnson delivered his State of the Union message. It is hardly necessary to remind ourselves that one of the reasons Americans and the British have not required a total immersion in the imagery of continental existentialism is that they had already found, in the early work of Eliot, an adequate description of not being at home in the world. We were all Prufrock before we had heard of Meersault.

Saul Bellow recently has written about the end of pessimism, and he has significantly spoken of the end of the Wasteland era, the end of the hollow men. Moses Herzog, in Bellow's novel, single-handedly takes on the whole fashionable pessimism of modern intellectual life. He lashes out against those who tell you how good dread is for you; he speaks of the "commonplaces of the Wasteland outlook, the cheap mental stimulants of Alienation, the cant and rant of pipsqueaks about Inauthenticity and Forlornness." Perhaps the most thoroughly post-modern, post-pessimistic act Herzog commits is his decision, at the close of the novel, not to go mad—his decision for human happiness. "I am pretty well satisfied to be, to be just as it is willed, and for as long as I may remain in occupancy."

Is it possible to note, some forty years after the publication of Eliot's *The Hollow Men,* that the world has ended neither with a bang nor a whimper? There was a period in the recent past when the fear of the bang was acute, but in spite of Vietnam today, America is not afraid, and it once more is beginning to take seriously the fact that it has a real future. Prufrock, the typist, the hollow men, never really connected with the real world; they were afraid of it. "In short, I was afraid." But on the night of Eliot's death, President Johnson invited his fellow countrymen not only to enter the world of the twentieth century but to accept the possibility of revolutionary changes in that world. Johnson's speech was just political rhetoric, one can say, and he would be correct. But it was somehow unlike political rhetoric of other eras—it was believable. And the legislative record of the first session—on domestic issues—has partly confirmed the rhetoric. This shift we are charting from pessimism to optimism can also be described as a move from alienation to politics, from blues to the freedom song.

There are three areas in which this change of sensibility, this move from pessimism to optimism, can be discerned—in the social sciences, in the field of art, and in the civil rights movement.

There is a good deal of very interesting avant-garde research in the social sciences being carried on in America, some of it in connection with universities, some of it not. Kenneth Boulding's recent book, *The Meaning of the Twentieth Century*, is an admirable example of this kind of work. Boulding describes the change of sensibility we've been describing. His point is that we are moving from a civilized to a post-civilized society, and that since civilized society is so disagreeable for so many, no tears should be lost as a result. The post-civilized age is the age of the mass media, of automation, of the constantly accelerating rate of change. The television show "Defenders" was civilized; "The Man from U.N.C.L.E." is post-civilized. Boulding's book describes the mood of those who are saying *yes* to the radical changes in our society, *yes* to techonology, *yes* to all the new and even threatening ways that man is finding to handle the world in which he lives. The atmosphere of the Conflict Resolution Center in Ann Arbor, where Boulding works, is one of a resolute confidence and optimism that even the really intractable problems that have marked our civilized period can be overcome, problems as apparently irreducible as war and mental illness.

Another example of technological optimism is to be found in the writing of Professor Marshall McLuhan and in the work of the Institute of Culture and Technology in Toronto. In his books and particularly in the recent *Understanding Media,* McLuhan delivers a vigorous indictment of the literate Western civilized man, busily engaged in rejecting the new media of communication and information-passing such as television. He claims, for example, that all media are extensions of our central nervous system, extensions of consciousness, rather like the psychodelic drugs. Because of this, he asserts, the process of knowing will very shortly be extended to the whole of human society, not merely to those we call educated in some limited sense. Since the media have so extended our consciousness of the whole world (*i.e.,* we no longer travel to see things, but to compare real things with pictures we have already seen), the era of the aloof, disinterested, liberal, scientific Western man is at an end. We are totally involved in everything that happens, and our goals, he says, are no longer control or mere understanding, but "wholeness, empathy, depth of awareness." (*Understanding Media,* p. 5)

The Negro and the teenager, for example, once could be isolated from the rest of society. They have become deeply involved with the rest of society and no longer can be pushed away. Television desegregates, as Bull Connor found out. This is what the media do; this is what the whole realm of automation technology does. It involves and unites, in contrast to the machine technology which separates and isolates.

McLuhan is to the post-civilized age, the electronic era, what Lewis Mumford has been to the mechanical age, with one striking difference. Mumford understood, but did not enjoy, the world the machine brought. McLuhan understands, delights in, and invites all men to delight in the new media of the post-civilized world.

Optimism in men like Boulding and McLuhan is related to acceptance of change, and even to creation of change. It is therefore an optimism about the future, and will remind some of the venerable doctrine of progress over which we have preached so many funeral orations. In their zest and optimism such men are still isolated voices, for complaints about the vulgarity and crudeness of a world moving too fast still predominate in intellectual circles. But these men, and a few others, see what is going on, and invite us to responsible and excited participation. Here, in the social sciences, is a radical "yes" to this century, an invitation to face, and a confidence that we can solve, some of our most difficult problems.

A recent essay by Lionel Trilling seems to belong with these developments. In his superb "The Two Environments" (included in the recent collection *Beyond Culture*) Trilling describes the moral climate within which the study of contemporary literature takes place in the American university today. Here, he finds, literature serves an almost religious function, placing before students not so much values or standards, but guides to the source of life, zest, and style. The contrast between Trilling's "first" and "second" environment, between moral seriousness (Matthew Arnold) and non-moral vitality (D. H. Lawrence), is very close to Boulding's distinction between civilized and post-civilized. And Trilling's moral criticism of some of the internal rules of the second environment—his attack on the over-valuation of literature and criticism and on alienation and despair as the artist's only gift to the moral life—parallels some of Bellow's recent concerns. This is a difficult and beautiful essay, and it is about the new America in which optimism is possible, the America in which the radical theology is trying to live.

There are some artistic movements today which point in the same direction—from pessimism to optimism. If one listens to the music of John Cage, for example, one engages a very articulate opponent of the modern tradition of art as self-expression, art as the imposition of the artist's selfhood and creativity on the chaos of experience. In this modern tradition art is work. It is serious, and it can be made to bear serious values. Cage rejects this tradition, and declares that the end of artistic creativity is not order or value but purposeless play, a play that affirms life and invites other men to wake up to the ordinary life around them that can be lived here and now. But for art to make this kind of invitation, the self and its desires must be removed. In some ways Cage represents an attack on the whole Renaissance conception of self-consciousness, and an adoption of a kind of secular-mystical idea of self as an enemy that must be removed before one can delight in the world for its own sake. Cage, and a number of others, represent an extensive revolt against modern, self-expressive art whose function is supposed to be that of uncovering or portraying the human condition. Art as selfless celebration or play is a very ancient concept of art, though it has been rather rare in the West since Goethe and romanticism. The theater of the absurd, the anti-novelists of France, some recent techniques in film-making, are all connected both by their protest against artistic self-expression and by their sharing this element of play or celebration in life.

One might almost say that the function of Cage's music is to remind people of the fact that every sound they hear is potentially music, if listened to in the right way. Every man, therefore, has the capacity to be his own artist and the materials of his art are simply the moments of his life as he lives it. Thus, if you say in response to some of Cage's indeterminate music, "My child could do that!", the proper answer is really, "Of course, so go home and teach him to do so!" Certain kinds of contemporary art—Robert Rauschenberg, in particular—show that the ordinary things which technological society rejects (Coke bottles, cans, old newspapers, tires) can be reassembled, with only the slightest nudges from the artist, into something gay and beautiful, and thus the whole of life can become the subject matter for such creativity.

Those who were lucky enough to be pulled or pushed, a year or so ago, to the Beatles' first movie, *A Hard Day's Night,* will recall the enchanting scene in which the four of them escape from the prison-like television studio, where worldly men are trying to get them to perform properly, and flee to an open field for a few surrealistic moments of jumping, dancing, abandon. This movie, and perhaps even the famous Beatles' sound, is part of this mood of celebration and rejoicing. In a review of the movie, the critic in the sombre *New Republic* (October 10,

1964) writes, "'A Hard Day's Night' floats above despair and alienation without ever challenging them head-on, but also without ignoring them."

Finally, in this sketchy list of movements toward optimism, the civil rights movement cannot be left out. It is, I think, my most decisive piece of evidence. That there is a gaiety, an absence of alienation, a vigorous and contagious hope at the center of this movement is obvious and this optimism is the main source of its hold on the conscience of America, particularly young America. You can most easily discern this optimism, beyond tragedy, beyond alienation, beyond existentialism, by singing the songs of the movement. If we think back to some of the great blues songs of the past, Bessie Smith's "Empty Bed Blues" for example, we hear no hope. The man is gone, he's not coming back, and the only healing is in the singing of the song. But when we listen to "We Shall Overcome" we have come into the world of historical optimism, in which this world is the place, and now is the time, for the making of the long-overdue changes.

We seem to be out of the fifties when the young were tame, safe, and cool, and when they explored, with guidebooks by J. D. Salinger and William Golding, the mysterious recesses of inner identity. The sixties may well be the time for play, celebration, delight, and for hope. A few years ago, Norman Podhoretz wrote about the young before the civil rights movement and the New Frontier rescued them from their inner preoccupations:

> Since this is a generation that willed itself from childhood directly into adulthood, it has still its adolescence to go through— for a man can never skip adolescence, he can only postpone it. And something very wonderful may come about when a whole generation in its late thirties breaks loose and decides to take a swim in the Plaza fountain in the middle of the night. (*Doings and Undoings*, p. 111.)

I think the prediction is coming true. Pessimism—political, theological, cultural—is coming to an end. The Plaza pool is crowded these nights.

The connection between the Plaza pool and Protestant theology has yet to be determined. What does theology make of this new optimism? In the thirties the cultural mood of anti-optimism drove men to rediscover Paul, Augustine, Kierkegaard. Does the new anti-pessimism simply compel us to look up some optimistic parts of the Christian tradition? Some would say so. Some are saying, and they may be right, that the life of Jesus with his disciples is the theological center of the new theology, just as Paul's struggle with the law was the center of the post-liberal development. This would mean that we would move from the "pessimism" of Paul to the eschatological optimism of the synoptics and thus give the new optimism a theological and biblical base. Something like this is already happening at those points where theological reflections on the civil rights movement are taking place.

The hunting up of biblical or theological foundations for something (in this case optimism) that has already taken place is not a thing I wish to do here. What are, if any, the theological reasons for this new optimism? We have, up to now, noted only a shift of sensibility, a shift due to cultural factors. I am persuaded, however, that in addition to cultural factors, the death of God has made this new optimism possible, and it is not an accident, but intended, deliberate, and natural, that the theologies of the death of God should be in themselves optimistic.

Perhaps the best way of showing the connection between the death of God and optimism is to note the central role that discussions of tragedy have taken in the intellectual world of pre-death of God theology. Neo-orthodoxy has talked a great deal about Christianity and tragedy, the possibility of Christian tragedy, the meaning of the tragic sense of life. More recently, a new point has been made. Not only are there no tragedies around—this could be described as an accident—but there can't be tragedies, many are saying. Why? Because the presence of tragedy requires the presence of God or the gods, and the presence of the gods is just what we do not have. The death of tragedy is due to the death of God.

God grew weary of the savagery of man. Perhaps he was no longer able to control it and could no longer recognize his image in the mirror of creation. He has left the world to its own inhuman devices and dwells now in some other corner of the universe so remote that his messengers cannot even reach us. I would suppose that he turned away during the seventeenth century. . . . In the nineteenth century, LaPlace announced that God was a hypothesis of which the rational mind had no further need; God took the great astronomer at his word. But tragedy is that form of art which requires the intolerable burden of God's presence. It is now dead because his shadow no longer falls upon us as it fell on Agamemnon or Macbeth or Athalie.

(George Steiner, *The Death of Tragedy*, p. 353)

We haven't had tragedy, Steiner claims, since the seventeenth century. It is not merely because men have not written them; it is also because there is no audience for them. Because, in other words, there are no tragic men either to create or to receive tragedy. And the disappearance of the tragic man is the consequence of the disappearance of the presence of God who makes tragedy possible.

Steiner's thesis is suggestive, but it needs refinement. It is much too simple, when we think of Romanticism and Deism for example, to talk about the disappearance of God in the seventeenth century. Even Nietzsche's madman confessed that his message of the death of God had come too soon. And if tragic man, in a rather narrow sense, did indeed disappear in the seventeenth century, some close relatives of his have continued down to our own time. Consider that very characteristic modern man, the man who fears his own death. Death is *the* tragic category, and death and the fear of death have been close to the center of modern sensibility for some time. Existentialist man and the man threatened by his own death—these are our modern comrades. They have not disappeared.

Steiner, I think, is wrong in his simple affirmation that the presence of tragedy and the tragic man requires the presence of God. Lucien Goldmann has seen the issue more clearly. What tragedy has always presupposed is not merely the divine presence, but a certain mixture of the divine presence and absence.

> The God of tragedy is a God who is always present and always absent. Thus, while his presence takes all value and reality from the world, his equally absolute and permanent absence makes the world into the only reality which man can confront, the only sphere in and against which he can and must apply his demand for substantial and absolute values.
>
> (*The Hidden God,* p. 50)

When tragic man experiences the presence of God, Goldmann says, the world is forgotten or devalued (it is worth noting here that Pascal and the Jansenism of Port Royal stands for tragic Christianity; Goldmann could hardly have assumed the unworldliness of the Christian man if he had focused on Calvin's elect man in the midst of the middle-class world), and when God is absent the world is remembered. Thus the world is both everything and nothing for the tragic man; it must never be abandoned for God; nor must God be abandoned for the world. The world cannot be changed; absolute values cannot be realized in it; the world can never satisfy tragic man. Why? Because the eye of God is always upon the tragic man, and the tragic man always returns from the world to the presence of God, even after long periods of absence. Thus, he can never really love or care for anything in the world, but can feel only longing and incompleteness in it. At this point, it would seem, the tragic man is virtually identical with religious man in the post-Reformation sense.

Goldmann is deeply influenced by Marx and the early Lukàcs and thus would agree that the tragic God of Pascal is dead. But unlike Steiner he does not think that tragic thought is dead. Modern man, instead of rescuing God from a permanent absence by means of a Pascalian wager, wagers instead on the human community, but he keeps his distance from this community, and never expects much from the world.

It seems to me that Steiner is right in insisting on the end of tragedy and tragic man, but wrong in simply identifying the death of tragedy in the seventeenth century with the death of God. I think Goldmann corrects Steiner when he points out that tragedy thrives not on the mere presence of God but on the dialectic between his presence and his absence.

The death of God, only hinted at in the seventeenth century, is the breakdown of the dialectic between the presence and absence. Absence has won a decisive victory over the presence. The madman predicted it, the plays of Ibsen work out the transformation of God into the conscience of man, and with Karl Marx the divine reality becomes the historical process. The greatest holdout in the nineteenth century was perhaps Dostoevsky, in whose very soul the struggle between the presence and the absence of God took a classical form. He was both Ivan and Alyosha.

> As far as I am concerned [Dostoevsky writes in a letter, March 1854], I look upon myself as a child of the age, a child of unbelief and doubt; it is probable, nay I know for certain, that I shall remain so to my dying day. I have been tortured with longing to believe—am so, indeed, even now; and the yearning grows stronger, the more cogent the intellectual difficulties that stand in the way.... And yet God sometimes sends me moments of complete serenity. It is in such moments that I have composed in my mind a profession of faith. ... This is what it is: to believe that there is nothing finer, deeper, more lovable, more reasonable, braver and more perfect than Christ; and, not only is there nothing, but I tell myself with a jealous love, there cannot be anything. More than that: if anyone had told me that Christ is outside truth, and if it had really been established that truth is outside Christ, I should have preferred to stay with Christ rather than with truth.

I have been concerned to establish a new mood of optimism in American culture. If I have seen this mood at all accurately, then we might be able to conclude that tragedy is culturally impossible, or unlikely. We trust the world, we trust the future, we deem even many of our intractable problems just soluble enough to reject the tragic mode of facing them. I am further adding to this descriptive argument that tragedy is theologically impossible, if it is the case that either the presence of God or the dialectic between the presence and absence are required. We do not have an equipoise between a having and a not-having; this was the equipoise of the neo-orthodox theology, the world of Dostoevsky's struggle, of existentialism and Prufrock and the rest. We are the not-havers, whose undialectical *yes* to the world is balanced by a *no* to God.

This is not an optimism of grace, but a worldly optimism I am defending. It faces despair not with the conviction that out of it God can bring hope, but with the conviction that the human conditions that created it can be overcome, whether those conditions be poverty, discrimination, or mental illness. It faces death not with the hope for immortality, but with the human confidence that man may befriend death and live with it as a possibility always alongside.

I think that the new optimism is both a cause and a consequence of the basic theological experience which we today call the death of God.

W. H.

By the spring of 1965 I began to fear that I would not find a publisher for my manuscript on Blake. The manuscript fits into no established category, insofar as it is a theological analysis of a strange body of prophetic poetry, employing Hegel as a dialectical guide to Blake's vision, and attempting to lay the groundwork for a new form of Christian theology. Herbert Weisinger had asked me to contribute an article to The Centennial Review *for an issue being devoted entirely to the problem of myth. Fearing that I could not easily come upon such a good opportunity for communicating some of my work on Blake, I selected a few crucial pages from my manuscript—guided in large measure by my wife's judgment— and added a few paragraphs on myth to make the result acceptable to Weisinger. The result was: "William Blake and the Role of Myth in the Radical Christian Vision."*

Somehow I love this piece more than any other article I have published, perhaps because of my love of Blake, but thus far its readers have reacted either with silence or with a mute but somehow meaningful affirmation.

T. J. J. A.

William Blake and the Role of Myth in the Radical Christian Vision

I

In rejecting the urgent plea that is made again and again in our day that we return to the sacred center of archaic myth, Herbert Weisinger justly notes that the history of myth has been the history of the demythologizing of myth. He then insists that any attempts to revive myth as a viable organ of belief are doomed to failure: "For we must remember that belief in myth is not a personal attainment alone; it is more, much more so, a social phenomenon and depends for its efficacy on group acceptance and adherence; a private myth, however admirably expressed in whatever form, is therefore an ultimate, irreconcilable contradiction." Few contemporary theologians would disagree with this statement, but we might well expect that many of Weisinger's brothers in arms, the literary critics, would raise a cry of protest against this seeming assault upon the reality of the individual mythical vision. Have we not learned in our century that the great poets are mythmakers or myth-transformers, that the forms of poetry are transmutations of archaic ritual forms, and that the poet symbol is an interiorization or a revalorization of the religious symbol? True, the modern poet—as exemplified, in widely divergent ways, by a Joyce and a Kafka—has given himself in large measure to a reversal of our mythical traditions. But is it not true, nevertheless, that the poetic vision is a form of the mythical vision?

Too many critics, both literary and theological, believe that at bottom the mythical vision is identical with the archaic vision, and thus they are persuaded that a mythical language can only be created and employed in the context of a primordial, a pre-historic, or a pre-rational human situation. Certainly a private myth must be an ultimate and irreconcilable contradiction if we assume that the mythmaker must be the priestly or ritual spokesman of a pre-literate society. Yet once granted that a genuine form of the mythical vision remains a possibility for civilized or historical man, and that myth itself is a creation of the human imagination, then it follows that a private myth is not only a possibility but is indeed the inevitable form by which a new or revolutionary myth will first appear in history.

The real issue at hand is whether or not there can be an individual and interior mythical vision, a vision that is not simply the reflection of an ancient mythical tradition, but a new creation, a vision that reflects and unveils a new form of the cosmos and history. All of us know that the old myths are dead. But does this mean that myth itself has died? Are we immersed in a world in which a total vision is no longer a possibility? Can myth in our time be no more than a dead fragment of the forgotten past or a pathological aberration of the sick mind? Or is the mythmaker in our seemingly post-Christian world doomed to be the gravedigger of the Christian God, the seer who can but name the darkness that has descended with the eclipse of our sun? Has the wheel now come full circle; must we return to the night of our beginning with no hope of another day? Have we lost the very power to name the darkness of our night? Ours is a situation that is peculiarly open to the vision of the most radical of all modern Christian visionaries, William Blake, for no poet or seer before him had so profoundly sensed the cataclysmic collapse of the cosmos created by Western man. Yet Blake celebrated this collapse as the way to a total and apocalyptic transfiguration of the world. Can Blake's vision be truly meaningful to us? Is the mythical world which he created one that can enter our consciousness and redirect our sensibility? Can we through Blake know a new form of the human hand and face, and a new direction of the vast cosmos about and beyond us? To the extent that these questions can be answered affirmatively we have a decisive means also of answering affirmatively the question of whether or not myth can assume a new and revolutionary form.

II

One cry is ever upon Blake's lips as he sings one song in myriad forms: "Awake! awake O sleeper of the land of shadows, wake; expand!" (*Jerusalem* 4:6). Man, the cosmos, reality itself—having fallen into division, generation, and decay—now sleep the sleep of eternal death. The fall is not a once and for all event, it is an eternal process, an eternal round of darkness and horror, even though that horror has assumed the illusory light of a fallen sun. Poets and prophets must name the horror; but the very act of naming stills its power, unveils its darkness, bringing light to darkness itself. Blake reveals that finally the poet and the prophet are one; the piper whose song brings joy to the child is the lamb whose pain both challenges and defies the tyrannic wheels of experience. If innocence and experience, the two contrary states of the human soul, must culminate in a common vision, then that vision must act upon that which it portrays. It must affect that which it reflects because vision is possible only by means of a transformation of its matter, a loosening of the stones that bind fallen man to his divided state. Poet and prophet must pronounce and act a No upon the world about and within them. Only on the basis of this No can authentic vision appear. The power and scope of vision depend inevitably upon the comprehensiveness of its rejection and reversal of experience. Blake, like his Old Testament prophetic forebearers, would appear to have spent his life and work in final no-saying; but that no-saying is dialectical. On its ground, and only on its ground, appears the yes-saying of apocalypse.

Just as Blake, the purest lyricist of English poetry, was destined by his very vision to become the most original seer in Christendom, so innocence must become experience, and the imagery of experience must reflect a night which has become all-encompassing, allowing no residue of light or purity to escape its awesome totality. Albion—Blake's symbol of the universal and cosmic "Man"—falls into the depths of darkness, and his fall is not only the fall of man but of all reality whatsoever. No God or heaven remains above or beyond this round of suffering and chaos, no realm of goodness or truth is immune to this universal process of descent, no primordial paradise or Eden remains open to ecstatic entry. In the light of Blake's vision, the fall is all, and, dialectically, the very fullness of his vision derives from the totality of its fallen ground: vision cannot reverse all things unless it initially knows them in a fallen form. An eschatological end can only follow a primordial beginning, but that beginning is not creation, it is fall. This is not fall as a primordial and distant event, but as a continual and present process, a process that has become identical with the very actuality of existence itself. Consequently we must not be appalled at the centrality of the image of the fall in Blake's work; we must not be dismayed that he very nearly succeeded in inverting all of the established categories of Western thought and experience. We must rather recognize that it is precisely this act of dialectical inversion which prepares the way for the apocalyptic vision of genuine faith. Faith is vision, proclaims Blake and every seer. But vision can neither arise nor be consummated apart from a transformation of the totality of experience. If faith is to become real in this final sense, it must ground itself in a dialectical reversal of everything which has passed through the "dark Satanic Mills" of history and the cosmos.

Blake's vision was ever circular and fluid. Characters and images move within and without his range in a perplexing manner; no real system is present in his work. Instead, we find a poetic or prophetic consistency arising from a series of dominant, if evasive, motifs. From the beginning, he rebelled against God, or against the God then present in Christendom, ironically disguising his attack by presenting him under the guise of a number of simple though powerful symbols, the most successful of which is surely the "Tyger." For the early Blake, the passionate rebel, God is the primary product and agent of repression, his law the deepest obstacle to liberty and joy. Yet the transcendent and wholly other God is not eternal; only when "Thought chang'd the infinite to a serpent" did God become a "tyrant crown'd" (*Europe* 10:16-23). The first chapter of *The Book of Urizen* opens with these lines:

> Lo, a shadow of horror is risen
> In Eternity! Unknown, unprolific,
> Self-clos'd, all-repelling; what Demon
> Hath form'd this abominable void,
> This soul-shudd'ring vacuum? Some said
> "It is Urizen." But unknown, abstracted,
> Brooding, secret, the dark power hid.

Here, Urizen appears as the Creator who, unseen and unknown, divides and measures space by space in his "ninefold darkness." Thus Urizen—or the Christian God—is a product of the fall. His very holiness, his *mysterium tremendum,* is created out of his dark solitude, where as he proclaims, "Here alone I" have written:

> "Laws of peace, of love, of unity,
> Of pity, compassion, forgiveness;
> Let each chuse one habitation,
> His ancient infinite mansion,
> One command, one joy, one desire,
> One curse, one weight, one measure,
> One King, one God, one Law."
> (*Book of Urizen* 4:34-40)

The figure of Urizen undergoes many transitions and transformations as Blake's vision unfolds, until he finally disappears in *Jerusalem.* Always, however, he is associated with the iron laws of the present creation, the repressive laws of morality, and the tyranny of governments and history. His realm is the icy and shadowy north, but his true abode is a solitary void, for the God who alone is God can only be evolved out of absolute solitude. Urizen is a peculiarly Blakean creation, and while he may initially have been little more than a parody of the Christian God, he gradually but surely brings to expression much of the fullness of Blake's pathos. Increasingly, Blake scholars are agreeing that in the period roughly between 1797 and 1807 Blake's work and vision underwent a decisive transformation.

During this period he wrote and rewrote and then finally abandoned *Vala* or *The Four Zoas,* he executed many of his most important paintings and designs, and he began engraving the plates for *Milton* and *Jerusalem.* As G. E. Bentley Jr.'s critical study of *Vala* demonstrates, Blake's frequent and disorderly revisions of this manuscript epic reveal his own movement into a Christian and redemptive understanding of history, an understanding that could not be reconciled with the initial direction of the poem. We have few clues to the personal ground of this transformation, the most important being a letter that Blake wrote to his patron, William Hayley, on October 23, 1804:

> For now! O Glory! and O Delight! I have entirely reduced that spectrous Fiend to his station, whose annoyance has been the ruin of my labours for the last passed twenty years of my life. . . . I speak with perfect confidence and certainty of the fact which has passed over me. . . . Suddenly, on the day after visiting the Truchessian Gallery of pictures, I was again enlightened with the light I enjoyed in my youth, and which has for exactly twenty years been closed from me as by a door and by window-shutters. . . . I thank God with entire confidence that it shall be so no longer—he is become my servant who domineered over me, he is even as a brother who was my enemy.

When we reflect that in this letter Blake is thanking God that he, Blake, has passed through a darkness that is presumably God's alone, we must be aware that we are confronting a theological paradox of the first order. Furthermore, at the conclusion of *The Four Zoas,* Urizen himself has been transposed into Satan, the Spectre or Selfhood of the mature Blake.

At this point we must fully recognize that Blake committed the blasphemy of blasphemies by identifying the biblical God as Satan. Not only did Blake leave numerous personal statements to this effect, but in his supreme pictorial creation, his illustrations for the Book of Job (and Blake, like Kierkegaard, ever identified himself with Job), he depicted God as Satan on the magnificent eleventh plate, and did so in fulfillment of his own vision, in this work, that redemption can take place only after the transcendent and numinous God has been recognized as Satan or Selfhood (*cf.* Joseph Wicksteed's study of the Job illustrations). Blake concludes *The Gates of Paradise* by addressing these words to Satan:

> Tho' thou art Worship'd by the Names Divine
> Of Jesus & Jehovah, thou art still
> The Son of Morn in weary Night's decline,
> The lost Traveller's Dream under the Hill.

This identification is a consistent motif throughout Blake's later work and it underlies his whole prophetic vision of the apocalypse. In *Milton,* Satan has taken on all of the former functions of Urizen, only here Satan does not declare "I am God Alone" until he establishes the law of repression (9:25). Now, Satan is the Spectre of Albion who made himself a God and destroyed the "Human Form Divine" (32:13); as such he is "Chaos" dwelling beyond the skies (20:33). This vision of God as Satan is consummated in *Jerusalem* where the Spectrous Chaos says to Albion, "that Human Form you call Divine is but a Worm," and then reveals that God is the "Great Selfhood, Satan" (33:1-24).

III

Although the identification of God as Urizen or Satan is a consistent and dominant theme of Blake's work, his later writings record a dark, if powerful, vision of a contrary motif, a vision of a kenotic movement in the Godhead leading to the redemption of a cosmic humanity. This vision arises in the context of a new and apocalyptic understanding of the "Mystery" of the Godhead. When Blake sees Satan within the dark Selfhood of Milton's shadow, he sees a "Human Wonder of God" reaching from heaven to earth, a "Human Form" revealing the monstrous Churches of a perverse innocence and the dark Gods of Hell (*Milton* 37:14-16). There follows an apocalyptic epiphany of these Gods in the twenty-seven heavens and their churches of the Antichrist. But in *Jerusalem* this epiphany is consummated in Jesus' triumphantly breaking through the central zones of death and Hell and opening eternity in time and space (*Jerusalem* 75:21).

With the dawn of the apocalypse God appears in his final form as Hell itself, for then he is fully incarnate as Ulro or Hell, and Jesus must break through that Hell to usher in eternity. This vision stands within the Christian theosophical tradition of Erigena, Boehme, and Schelling, with its witness to the dialectical and historical movements of the Godhead. Blake's vision is more consistently kenotic, for it fully identifies God with the dark abyss or evil potency of the Godhead even while unveiling the goal of this potency as being wholly redemptive. If the young Blake delighted in greeting Satan as a redemptive figure, and an older Blake was overwhelmed and almost crushed by a realization of the deeper consequences of the divine identity of Satan, the regenerate Blake was finally able to name Satan as Jesus, thereby unveiling the redemptive goal of the fallen world of experience.

Blake was an apostle to the Gentiles, and his message brings forth the same offense in his readers that is always induced by an authentic proclamation of the Gospel. That offense is most deeply present in Blake's devotion to "Jesus only" (the motto of *Jerusalem*), in his call to all mankind to accept the goal of becoming identical with Jesus, and in his conviction that Jesus is the "Universal Humanity." If only because of his faith in Jesus we must acknowledge that Blake is a Christian seer, but he is by far the most Christocentric of Christian visionaries, despite the fact that his revolutionary vision of Jesus arose out of a rebellion against the "Christian Christ."

Why should Blake have given such reverence to the name of Jesus? Why believe that Jesus' passion is present throughout history, that Jesus is the lamb who is slain in all his children, and that only Jesus can save us from our destructive Selfhood? How could one who was so overwhelmingly committed to the universal redemption of humanity make such absolute claims for a particular historical figure? Moreover, the actual name of Jesus was every bit as sacred to Blake as it is to those Eastern practitioners of Hesychism who pronounce the name of Jesus as the path to salvation. This is because Jesus' name has an historical actuality for the Christian—even for so radical a Christian as Blake—that is matched by no other. True, such names as Krishna and Kali, and Amithabba and Avalokitesvara, have a comparable redemptive power to the bhakti Hindu and Buddhist; but bhakti religion, whether in its Christian or non-Christian forms, has an inevitable tendency to dissociate the sacred name from the actualities of concrete experience. Blake passionately resisted this transformation of experience into innocence, and while he could not always withstand the temptations of a traditional Christian imagery and iconography, he did so in his greatest vision (*e.g.*, the face of Jesus is not present in the designs of *Jerusalem*). No doubt the name of Jesus will disappear in the apocalypse, and the radical or spiritual Christian need have no reason to believe that it must be employed by the non-Christian; yet the reality underlying his name is the innermost reality of the Christian faith.

Already in the *Songs of Innocence* there is an underlying vision of the omnipresence of the passion of Jesus, and as Blake gradually but decisively came to see that passion in every concrete pain and sorrow, he was prepared to celebrate the naked horror of experience as an epiphany of the crucified lamb of God. "Experience," as Milton O. Percival says, "is with Blake the essence of regeneration." But experience is found only in the fallen world of generation, a world that Blake symbolically associated with the loins, since the very purpose of generation is its gift of life. Having long believed that everything that lives is holy, Blake finally came to see the world of generation as the incarnate body of Christ:

"O holy Generation, Image of regeneration!
O point of mutual forgiveness between Enemies!
Birthplace of the Lamb of God incomprehensible!
The Dead despise & scorn thee & cast thee out as accursed,
Seeing the Lamb of God in thy gardens & thy palaces
Where they desire to place the Abomination of Desolation."

(*Jerusalem* 7:65-70)

Generation, as the fullness of passion that is present in sexual energy, is not simply the source of life, but in its own form and direction is the temporal image of the process of redemption. Consequently, generation will not have fulfilled its function until it makes Christ manifest in the fullness of experience. Experience itself, therefore, is only truly consummated in the passion of generation where the spontaneous expression of bodily energy duplicates and even makes incarnate in each individual body the universal process of the *kenosis* or emptying of the Godhead. The lamb of God sports in the gardens of sexual delight because these gardens are palaces of self-annihilation and mutual forgiveness. The ecstasy of liberation that is the gift of sex reverses the repressed energy of a fallen body, and resurrects the dead who are enslaved to an alien law and an inhuman Creator. Yet Satan has sealed the process of generation in a veil of repression; the sheer immediacy of delight has passed under condemnation and become the very essence of the forbidden, as the "Abomination of Desolation" has been erected in the temple of Christ. Therefore the Incarnation will not be complete until the body of Satan is transformed into Jerusalem, for then the passion of Jesus will appear in its full form as a regenerate experience.

Paradoxically, sexual generation simultaneously appears in Blake's vision both as the repressed product of Satan's "mills" and as the most immediate arena of the process of regeneration. Jesus, who is the incarnation of the primordial passion of "Luvah," is at once the dark body of Satan and the redemptive body of holiness:

> "A Vegetated Christ & a Virgin Eve are the Hermaphroditic
> Blasphemy; by his Maternal Birth he is that Evil-One
> And his Maternal Humanity must be put off Eternally,
> Lest the Sexual Generation swallow up Regeneration.
> Come Lord Jesus, take on thee the Satanic Body of Holiness!"
> (*Jerusalem* 90:34-38)

Despite those critics who cite this fragment of Blake's vision as evidence of a Gnostic hatred of the body, we have only to recall his continual and ecstatic celebration of sexuality and the body to recognize these lines as containing a vision of the regeneration and reversal of a fallen sexuality. The hermaphroditic blasphemy is a generated or vegetated Christ *and* a virgin Eve—the orthodox image of Christ, for the Church castrated Jesus when it locked the memory of his generation in the image of a virgin birth, just as it dehumanized and falsely spiritualized his body in its belief in the ascension. Yet Jesus continually reverses his "Maternal Humanity" by becoming incarnate in a satanic body of holiness. His very existence in a generated body challenges Satan's repression and initiates the process of reversing the fallen energy of the body. This movement of reversing the world of experience is the process of regeneration, and it occurs only in the full actuality of the body. For the living energy of the body is not only the image of regeneration, but is itself the most immediate manifestation of the incarnate body of Jesus. What the Church knows as the descent of Christ into Hell is not, according to Blake's vision, a descent apart from the body, but rather a descent into the very depths of bodily repression, a descent that is only consummated in the identification of Jesus' "Satanic Body of Holiness" with the totality of the cosmos, and its consequent presence as the redemptive fire of passion throughout the whole body of humanity.

For the first time in the history of Christian imagery, Blake has given the world a dynamic image of the cosmic Christ. Blake's "atheism" was not simply a prophetic reaction to the appearance in his time of a non-redemptive God of power and judgment, but more deeply was a radical Christian response to a divine sovereignty that stands apart from the kenotic movement of the Incarnation. By coming to know the total presence of God in the Incarnation, Blake and every radical Christian is liberated from the God who is wholly other than man, and likewise liberated from the authority of a heteronomous law and an autonomous Creator. To the spiritual or radical Christian, the very name of Jesus not only symbolizes but also makes actually present the total union of God and man, and for that reason it likewise gives witness to a concrete reversal of history, and a dawning apocalyptic transfiguration of the cosmos. The name of Jesus embodies the promise of these final things while simultaneously calling for a "Self-annihilation" that issues in a total identification with our neighbor. Truly to pronounce his name is to give oneself to Jesus as he is manifest in the weak and broken ones about us, and as he is present in the darkness, the anonymity, and the chaos of a fallen history. Consequently, Blake reveals that a fully Christian repetition of the name of Jesus annuls those empty spaces separating man from man, and man from God. The passion of Jesus is the fulfillment of the solitary and transcendent God's kenotic movement into man; the Jesus whom Blake names as the seventh eye of God comes and freely dies to reverse God's distant and satanic form. God himself passes through "Self-annihilation" in Jesus' passion, and, as a result of that passion, and by repeating Jesus' passion in the actuality of experience, the Christian can discover a new and joyous humanity, a humanity that is born only by means of the death of God: "Thou art a Man, God is no more" (*The Everlasting Gospel*).

Blake proclaims the Jesus whose redemptive presence makes present once again the actuality of the death of God. With the death of God every alien law and authority has been stripped of its foundation, the spaces separating man from man have been bridged, and the irreversibility of past moments of time has been annulled.

> Jesus said: "Wouldest thou love one who never died
> For thee, or ever die for one who had not died for thee?
> And if God dieth not for Man & giveth not himself
> Eternally for Man, Man could not exist; for Man is Love
> As God is Love: every kindness to another is a little Death
> In the Divine Image, nor can Man exist but by brotherhood."
> (*Jerusalem* 96:23-28)

We exist as "Man" only by knowing that God is love. Yet we only know his love by knowing the presence of Jesus, a presence wherein God eternally dies for man; and by practicing the reality of God's love as mediated through Jesus, we ourselves effect the death of God. The God who eternally dies for man is the God who is kenotically incarnate in every alien other. His dying dissolves that other, and his death in Jesus initiates the apocalypse. Once God has died in Jesus, he is present only in Jesus' resurrected body, and that body is the cosmic body of a new humanity. No way to this body is present in the memories and traditions of the Church—for the Church can only know the past and particular body of Jesus, the crucified body in the tomb, since the Lord of the ascension has negated the human and living body of Jesus. The new body that is created by Jesus' passage into death—by the voluntary death of God in Jesus—is the body of the incarnate God who has totally identified himself with experience.

Finally, Blake's Christian vision reveals that Jesus is the name of the totality of experience, an experience that is born with the abolition of repression, and that is potentially present wherever there is life. Jesus is the "Eternal Vision," the "Divine Similitude," which if man ceases to behold, he ceases to exist:

> "Mutual in one another's love and wrath all renewing
> We live as One Man; for contracting our infinite senses
> We behold multitude, or expanding we behold as one,
> As One Man all the Universal Family, and that One Man
> We call Jesus the Christ. . . ."
>
> *(Jerusalem* 38:16-20)

Truly to pronounce the name of Jesus is to pierce the darkness of a fallen condition and to give witness to the ultimately human reality of experience. The Blake who declares that God is Jesus (Laocoon engraving) is the Blake who envisioned an experience that is totally fallen and totally human at once. Jesus is the name of the God who has become totally incarnate in experience—even unto death—and his death has been consummated in the advent of "The Great Humanity Divine." Perhaps only a poet would have dared to speak of "The Great Humanity Divine" as Los or the human imagination:

> Then Jesus appeared standing by Albion as the Good Shepherd
> By the lost Sheep that he hath found, & Albion knew that it

Was the Lord, the Universal Humanity; & Albion saw his Form
A Man, & they conversed as Man with Man in Ages of Eternity.
And the Divine Appearance was the likeness & similitude of Los.

(*Jerusalem* 96:3-7)

IV

William Blake is the only poet ever to have created an apocalypse or a fully apocalyptic work of art—for, according to Northrop Frye, *Milton* and *Jerusalem* are inseparable, and constitute a "double epic," a prelude and fugue on the same subject. When we reflect that the original message of Jesus was an eschatological proclamation of the dawning of the Kingdom of God, that the patristic Church transformed this message by a dissolution and elimination of its apocalyptic ground, that, ever since, the dogmatic and ritual foundations of the orthodox Church have been non-apocalyptic, and that it has only been in the non-verbal arts that Christendom has produced an apocalyptic imagery, then on this ground alone we would be fully justified in pronouncing Blake to be a revolutionary artist and seer. To understand the theological significance of this fact, we must first draw together those points at which Blake is a unique Christian visionary. Upon careful analysis, at least ten such points become apparent: (1) Blake alone among Christian artists has created a whole mythology; (2) he was the first to discover the final loss of paradise, the first to acknowledge that innocence has been wholly swallowed up by experience; (3) no other Christian artist or seer has so fully directed his vision to history and experience; (4) to this day his is the only Christian vision that has openly or consistently accepted a totally fallen time and space as the paradoxical presence of eternity; (5) he stands alone among Christian artists in identifying the actual passion of sex as the most immediate epiphany of either a demonic or a redemptive "Energy," just as he is the only Christian visionary who has envisioned the universal role of the female as both a redemptive and a destructive power; (6) his is the only Christian vision of the total kenotic movement of God or the Godhead; (7) he was the first Christian "atheist," the first to unveil God as Satan; (8) he is the most Christocentric of Christian seers and artists; (9) only Blake has created a Christian vision of the full identity of Jesus with the individual human being (the "minute particular"); and (10) as the sole creator of a post-biblical Christian apocalypse, he has given Christendom its only vision of a total cosmic reversal of history.

Of course, Blake belongs to a large company of radical or spiritual Christians, Christians who believe that the Church and Christendom have sealed Jesus in his tomb and resurrected the very evil and darkness that Jesus conquered by their exaltation of a solitary and transcendent God, a heteronomous and compulsive law, and a salvation history that is irrevocably past. Despite its great relevance to our situation, the faith of the radical Christian continues to remain largely unknown, and this is so both because that faith has never been able to speak in the established categories of Western thought and theology and because it has so seldom been given a visionary expression (or, at least, the theologian has not been able to understand the radical vision, or even perhaps to identify its presence). It can be said, however, that the radical Christian invariably attempts by one means or another to return to the original message and person of Jesus with the conviction that such a return demands both an assault upon the established Church and a quest for a total or apocalyptic redemption. Here, everything depends upon the meaning of an apocalyptic redemption. Its original meaning was certainly lost in the long history of Christendom, and the radical Christian faces the task not only of discovering that meaning, but of mediating it in a new and "spiritual" form to his own time and situation.

A revealing light can now be cast upon the problem of the distinctive meaning of an apocalyptic faith by comparing that faith—particularly as it is present in the radical Christian—with the higher religious expressions of mysticism. Fundamentally, the purer forms of mysticism effect an interior dissolution of that experience which has accrued to man in the course of his history, abolishing thereby both man's autonomous selfhood and his attachment to all exterior reality, and leading simultaneously to a total identification with and immediate participation in an all-encompassing ultimate Reality. Oriental mysticism, particularly in its Indian forms, knows this ultimate Reality as an absolute quiescence, although this quiescence is apprehended as a cosmic Totality. Moreover, this Totality is a primordial Reality; it is both the underlying identity of all reality, and the original form of the cosmos. Therefore, the way of Oriental mysticism is a way *backwards* to the primordial beginning. While this original Totality comprehends and in fact unifies all those antinomies that have evolved in the course of the history or movement of the cosmos, it remains an eternal and unmoving Totality which at bottom has never ceased to be itself. It could even be said that Oriental mysticism must identify movement as the source of the "fall": only through the advent of motion, process, and energy does the cosmos assume a fallen form, despite the fact that neither movement nor the "fall" can here be judged to be ultimately real.

Now it is precisely at this point that we must acknowledge a seemingly unbridgeable gulf between the worlds of Oriental mysticism and Biblical eschatology. Eschatological faith is the expression of an immediate participation in the "Kingdom of God"—an apocalyptic symbol that was never assimilated by Christian theology. But that "Kingdom" is a dynamic epiphany of a Godhead in process of realizing itself. So far from existing as a static and timeless Totality, here the Godhead appears and is real only insofar as it is an active process of negating the fallen form of history and the cosmos. An eschatological faith that celebrates the "dawning" of the Kingdom of God cannot know the God who alone is God, just as it cannot know an inactive and quiescent Godhead. The God whom it proclaims is present solely in his Kingdom, and that Kingdom is a forward-moving process effecting an absolute transformation of the world. Consequently, the way of eschatological faith is a way *forwards* to an ultimate and final Eschaton, and that Eschaton is a once-and-for-all decisive event which will be both a fulfillment of the total movement of the Godhead and a realization of a final paradise which must wholly transcend the paradise of the beginning.

Hopefully we should now be in a position to ascertain something of the meaning both of an apocalyptic faith and of a poetic apocalypse which embodies that faith in a concrete expression. Such a faith revolves about a response to the advent of the final Eschaton; it must be a total response to reflect the all-encompassing finality of the Eschaton, for it knows God's acts as being already present. These acts are present solely in a dynamic and forward-moving process that even now is reversing the totality of history and the cosmos, and therefore effecting an absolute transformation of a Totality that is human, cosmic, and divine. Only by abandoning its original faith in the dawning Kingdom of God that is in actual process of realizing itself could orthodox Christianity arrive at its belief in the transcendent and solitary God who is the Wholly Other. When the reality of God is eschatologically identified with his dawning Kingdom, then God can be known only as an active and apocalyptic process that even now is becoming all in all.

Apocalyptic faith is the inevitable expression of an immediate and total participation in the dawning "Kingdom." It must reflect a cosmic reversal that is bringing an "end" to the world, and thus it must give witness to a forward-moving process that is transforming the foundations of the cosmos. An authentic witness to the meaning of this process must incorporate a vision of a world that is ceasing to be itself, of a Godhead that is kenotically becoming its own Other, and of a new humanity that is passing into the final paradise. This is precisely the function of a poetic apocalypse. Accordingly, such an apocalypse must be an imaginative disclosure of a universal and kenotic process that moves through an absolute and total negation to reach the epiphany of a divine and human Totality that thereby becomes all in all.

Blake and every radical Christian seer have not only issued a violent protest against the "Christian God," but they have likewise condemned the mystery and repression of religion as a fundamental obstacle to the realization of a union with the life and Word of Jesus. While the radical Christian tends to identify "religion" with the established beliefs and practices of the Christian Church, it is nonetheless true that a new form of Christianity appears in the radical Christian which establishes a new and deeper gulf between Christianity itself and the world of non-Christian religion. If we allow Blake's apocalyptic vision to stand witness to a radical Christian faith, there are at least seven points from within this perspective at which we can discern the uniqueness of Christianity: (1) a realization of the centrality of the fall and of the totality of fallenness throughout the cosmos; (2) the fall in this sense cannot be known as a negative or finally illusory reality, for it is a process or movement that is absolutely real while yet being paradoxically identical with the process of redemption; and this because (3) faith, in its Christian expression, must finally know the cosmos as a kenotic and historical process of the Godhead's becoming incarnate in the concrete contingency of time and space; (4) insofar as this kenotic process becomes consummated in death, Christianity must celebrate death as the path to regeneration; (5) so likewise the ultimate salvation that will be effected by the triumph of the Kingdom of God can take place only through a final cosmic reversal; (6) nevertheless, the future Eschaton that is promised by Christianity is not a repetition of the primordial beginning, but is a new and final paradise in which God will have become all in all; and (7) faith, in this apocalyptic sense, knows that God's Kingdom is already dawning, that it is present in the words and person of Jesus, and that only Jesus is the "Universal Humanity," the final coming together of God and man.

Just as the full meaning of Blake's vision continues to elude his contemporary interpreter, so, too, the theologian has yet to unravel both the foundations and the implications of a radical Christian faith. One conclusion, however, is inescapable: a new form of faith is present in the radical Christian, a form that seemingly inverts its orthodox counterpart, and which yet claims to be a recovery and renewal of the original message and person of Jesus. Both the secular and the priestly mind will no doubt continue to identify this radical faith as "atheistic," yet no responsible judgment could deny that radical Christianity does embody a strange rebirth of the long lost eschatological foundations of Christianity.

A fundamental issue here has to do with the identity of Christianity. Has Christianity for all time been given to the apostles and the guardians of faith? Must Christianity be identified with its given or orthodox dogmatic form? Are we bound to confine the Christian "myth" to its past historical expressions? Yet we must notice that the very form of these questions gives evidence of a non-Christian conception of religion. Such questions simply assume that there is a single essence of faith, that this essence is present in the past, and that faith itself is the remembrance or repetition of a past or primordial reality. Conceived in this sense, faith is identified as a backward-movement or return to a primordial beginning or an original paradise. Blake knew this original paradise of innocence as a paradise lost, and for that reason he passionately opposed "remembrance," and understood it as being the very antithesis of faith or vision. The specifically apocalyptic or eschatological ground of the Christian faith demands that it be a forward-moving process revolving about the absolute negation of the old cosmos of a totally fallen history. In *Jerusalem,* Blake names this absolute negation a "Fourfold Annihilation," a total annihilation that is "going forward, forward irresistible from Eternity to Eternity" (98:27). Indeed, the radical Christian has taken this original ground of the Christian faith to its inevitable fulfillment: if all eternity must pass through "Self-Annihilation," then God himself must die to make possible the redemptive triumph of the apocalypse, for his death reverses that "Self-hood" which is the source of the fall.

A form of faith or belief that adheres to an unmoving and immobile Godhead must deny the possibility of a forward-movement "from Eternity to Eternity," just as it must submit to the absolute sovereignty of the primordial God. When faith is understood in this sense, there can be no question of a transformation of faith itself in response to the movement of the Godhead. But an apocalyptic and radical form of the Christian faith celebrates a cosmic and historical movement of the Godhead that culminates in the death of God himself. Blake named God as Urizen or Satan at the very moment when he discovered the apocalyptic significance of the death of the Christian God—

as witness his first prophetic poem, *America*. Only when the passion of Jesus has been consummated in the epiphany of the death of God in the concrete actuality of history does God himself appear in his apocalyptic form as a dying Satan:

> Over the hills, the vales, the cities, rage the red flames fierce:
> The Heavens melted from north to south: and Urizen, who sat
> Above all heavens, in thunders wrap'd, emerg'd his leprous head
> From out his holy shrine, his tears in deluge piteous
> Falling into the deep sublime: flag'd with grey-brow'd snows
> And thunderous visages, his jealous wings wav'd over the deep;
> Weeping in dismal howling woe, he dark descended, howling
> Around the smitten bands, clothed in tears & trembling, shudd'ring cold.
> His stored snows he poured forth, and his icy magazines
> He open'd on the deep. . . .
>
> (*America* 16:2-10)

While this vision represents only the initial phase of Blake's apocalyptic work, it nevertheless records a new and decisive image of God—an image that prophetically foreshadows Moby Dick—and an image that itself reflects a new moment of redemptive history, a moment in which God himself passes into a satanic form and finally dies as Satan to make possible the cosmic reversal of the apocalypse. How are we to judge this image of God? It is not wholly the product of a "private mythology," for it is rooted in a history as old as Gnosticism, and it anticipates the whole world of the modern vision. If we are to speak theologically, must we not finally say that this image of God as Satan is either itself a satanic and all too modern form of deicide, or else a new and radical form of the Christian faith?

As one who accepted the strange vocation of being an apocalyptic seer, Blake was not in quest of a hidden but ancient mythical form; instead, he was engaged in a desperate search for a new mythical "system" by which he might record the dawning of a final movement of redemption in the arena of our totally fallen history. To insist that Blake was successful as an artist and poet only to the extent that he resurrected an ancient form of myth is to deny the Christian ground of his vision and to reject the great bulk of his mature work. If we must refuse all that is new in Blake's vision, then we must simply repudiate Blake as an artist and seer. Blake was the first of the great modern seers. Through Blake we can sense the theological significance of a poetic reversal of our mythical traditions, and become open to the possibility that the uniquely modern metamorphosis of the sacred into the profane is the culmination of a redemptive and kenotic movement of the Godhead. The Blake who proclaimed that God must eternally die for man, that a primordial Totality must pass through "Self-Annihilation," was the Blake who envisioned a uniquely contemporary Christ, a Christ who becomes Antichrist before he is resurrected as Jerusalem.

The closing pages of *Jerusalem* record a vision of a coming apocalyptic *coincidentia oppositorum,* revealing how the final union of God and man will annihilate the God who alone is God by resurrecting him as "The Great Humanity Divine." Every fragment of ecstatic joy and bodily delight foreshadows this union, every momentary death of selfhood negates a barrier to this apocalyptic reversal, every affirmation of an opposing other sanctifies that Satan who will ultimately be transfigured into Jerusalem. Finally, Albion will become a radiant Jerusalem, a new cosmos appearing as the "Humanity Divine," an Eden who will be "One Man." Dare the contemporary Christian reject this vision? Or is he doomed to cling to a dead image of Jesus, even at the cost of life?

T. J. J. A.

Bibliography

Selected list of works pertaining to the radical development in theology, prepared by William Hamilton.

I. ENLIGHTENMENT RELIGIOUS THOUGHT

Radical theology has some affinity with both the critical and constructive projects of Enlightenment theology, and some would mark the French Revolution as the true beginning of radical theology.

Cassirer, Ernst. *The Philosophy of the Enlightenment*. Princeton: Princeton University Press, 1951.

Gay, Peter. *The Party of Humanity: Essays in the French Enlightenment*. New York: Knopf, 1963.

Hazard, Paul. *European Thought in the Eighteenth Century*. Cleveland: World, 1964. *See* Part I; Part II, chaps. 4, 5; Part III, book 3.

Manuel, Frank (ed.). *The Enlightenment*. Englewood Cliffs, N. J.: Prentice-Hall, 1965. *See* Part II: Religion and Superstition.

———. *The Prophets of Paris: Turgot, Condorcet, Saint-Simon, Fourier, Comte*. New York: Harper, 1965.

II. SOME NINETEENTH CENTURY BACKGROUND MATERIAL

A. *General surveys of the period*

Barth, Karl. *From Rousseau to Ritschl*. London: SCM Press, 1959.

Croce, Benedetto. *History of Europe in the Nineteenth Century*. New York: Harcourt, Brace and World, 1963.

Löwith, Karl. *From Hegel to Nietzsche*. New York: Holt, Rinehart & Winston, 1964.

B. *The Hegelian left*

Feuerbach, Ludwig. *The Essence of Christianity*. Introduction by Karl Barth. New York: Harper, 1957.

Fromm, Erich. *Marx's Concept of Man*. New York: Ungar, 1961.

Halle, Louis. "Marx's Religious Drama," *Encounter*, October, 1965.

Hegel, G. W. F. *Phenomenology of Mind*. New York: Humanities.

———. *Science of Logic*. Translated by W. H. Johnson and L. G. Struthers. New York: Humanities.

Hook, Sidney. *From Hegel to Marx*. Ann Arbor: Michigan, 1962.

Marx, Karl and Friedrich Engels. *On Religion*. New York: Schocken, 1964.

Strauss, David F. *Life of Jesus*. Translated by George Eliot. 4th Edition.

Tucker, Robert. *Philosophy and Myth in Karl Marx*. New York and London: Cambridge, 1964.

C. *The early work of Schleiermacher belongs in any list of the theological roots of radical theology. See especially*

Schleiermacher, Friedrich. *On Religion*. New York: Harper, 1958.

D. *Literary expressions of radical religious thought*

1. William Blake

Blake, William. "The Everlasting Gospel," "Marriage of Heaven and Hell," "Jerusalem," and "Milton," *The Poetry and Prose of William Blake*. Edited by Harold Bloom and David V. Erdman. New York: Doubleday, 1965.

Frye, Northrop. *Fearful Symmetry*. Boston: Beacon Press, 1962.

2. Heinrich Heine

Heine, Heinrich. *Religion and Philosophy in Germany*. Boston: Beacon Press, 1959. *See* page 103 for reference to death of God.

3. Fyodor Dostoevsky

Dostoevsky, Fyodor. *Notes from the Underground*. New York: New American Library.

———. *The Brothers Karamazov*. New York: Vintage.

———. *The Idiot*. New York: Modern Library.

———. *The Possessed*. New York: New American Library, 1962.

Wellek, Rene. *Dostoevsky, A Collection of Critical Essays*. Englewood Cliffs, N. J.: Prentice-Hall, 1962.

4. Leo Tolstoy

Radical theology is interested in the unconventional religious views of writers in the nineteenth century. Tolstoy's religious thought can best be studied in the following books:

Tolstoy, Leo. *Anna Karenina*. New York: Norton, 1965.

————. *The Kingdom of God Is Within You.* New York: Noonday, 1905.

————. *On Life, and Essays on Religion.* London and New York: Oxford.

5. Matthew Arnold

Arnold is an excellent example of the struggle of belief and unbelief in Victorian England.

Arnold, Matthew. *God and the Bible.* New York: Macmillan, 1893.

————. *Literature and Dogma.* Boston: James R. Osgood and Co., 1873.

The following books are useful for a study of the religious thought of nineteenth century literary England.

Buckley, Vincent. *Poetry and Morality.* New York: Humanities Press, 1964.

Miller, Joseph Hillis. *The Disappearance of God: Five Nineteenth Century Writers.* Cambridge: Harvard University Press, 1963.

Shafer, Robert. *Christianity and Naturalism.* New Haven: Yale University Press, 1928.

Trilling, Lionel. *Matthew Arnold.* New York: Norton, 1939.

Willey, Basil. *Nineteenth Century Studies.* New York: Columbia University Press, 1949.

6. American Literature

Radical theology is examining its roots in American thought of the nineteenth century, as well as European, and to this end works in the general area of American studies will be useful:

Baritz, Loren. *City on a Hill.* New York: Wiley, 1964.

McDermott, John J. "The American Angle of Vision," *Cross Currents,* Spring, 1965 and Fall, 1965.

Marx, Leo. *The Machine in the Garden.* New York: Oxford University Press, 1964.

Matthiessen, F. O. *American Renaissance.* New York: Oxford University Press, 1941.

Thompson, L. *Melville's Quarrel with God.* Princeton: Princeton University Press, 1952.

Twain, Mark. "Reflections on Religion," Charles Neider (ed.) in *The Hudson Review,* Autumn, 1963.

E. *Friedrich Nietzsche*

Nietzsche, Friedrich. "The Antichrist" and "The Gay Science,"

Nietzsche: An Anthology of His Works. New York: Washington Square Press, 1964.

―――. *Thus Spoke Zarathustra.* Translated by R. J. Hollingdale. Baltimore: Penguin Books, 1961.

―――. "Twilight of the Idols," *The Portable Nietzsche.* Edited and translated by Walter Kaufmann. New York: Viking, 1954.

Some recent secondary sources:

Fischer, Kurt. "The Existentialism of Nietzsche's Zarathustra," *Daedalus,* Summer, 1964.

Heller, Erich. "The Importance of Nietzsche," *Encounter,* April, 1964.

Jaspers, Karl. *Nietzsche.* Tucson: University of Arizona Press, 1965.

―――. *Nietzsche and Christianity.* Chicago: Gateway, 1961.

III. TYPES OF MODERN RADICAL RELIGIOUS THOUGHT

A. *Religious philosophies without God*

Dewey, John. *A Common Faith.* New Haven: Yale University Press, 1964.

Santayana, George. *Reason in Religion.* New York: Scribner's, 1906.

Wieman, Henry Nelson. *The Source of Human Good.* Chicago: University of Chicago Press, 1946.

There is a connection between radical theology and the religious liberalism of the Unitarian and Universalist traditions and a connection with humanism. *See*

Huxley, Julian. *Religion Without Revelation.* New York: Mentor, 1958.

Krutch, Joseph Wood. *The Modern Temper.* New York: Harcourt, Brace, 1929. *See* passage on the death of God, pp. 9-10.

B. *Roman Catholic scholarship*

There is a contemporary school of theological interpretation of atheism which is largely Roman Catholic.

Borne, Etienne. *Atheism.* New York: Hawthorne, 1961.

Chenu, M. D. and Friedrich Heer. "Is the Modern World Atheist?" *Cross Currents,* Winter, 1961.

Gorres, Ida. "The Believer's Unbelief," *Cross Currents,* Winter, 1961.

Lacroix, Jean Paul. *The Meaning of Modern Atheism.* New York: Macmillan, 1965.

Lepp, Ignace. *Atheism in Our Time*. New York: Macmillan, 1963.

Maritain, Jacques. "On the Meaning of Contemporary Atheism," *The Review of Politics*, July, 1949.

Novak, Michael. *Belief and Unbelief*. New York: Macmillan, 1965.

Rahner, Karl. "Wissenschaft als Konfession?" *Wort und Wahrheit*, November, 1954.

Smith, F. J. "Christianity and Christ," *American Church Quarterly*, iv, No. 4, Winter, 1964.

von Balthasar, Hans Urs. *Science, Religion and Christianity*. London: Burns and Oates, 1958.

See also the following title for a Protestant viewpoint:

Marty, Martin. *Varieties of Unbelief*. New York: Holt, Rinehart, 1964.

C. *Modern literary figures who have dealt specifically, if unconventionally, with religious themes*

Gide, André. *Journals*. 4 vols. New York: Knopf, 1951. *See* especially vol. ii, pp. 169 ff., and vol. iii, pp. 370 ff.

D. H. Lawrence, works on:

Goodheart, Eugene. "Lawrence and Christ," *Partisan Review*, Winter, 1964.

Krook, Dorothea. *Three Traditions of Moral Thought*. New York: Cambridge University Press, 1959.

Spilka, Mark. *The Love Ethic of D. H. Lawrence*. Bloomington, Ind.: Indiana University Press, 1955.

Tiverton, William (Martin Jarrett-Kerr). *D. H. Lawrence and Human Existence*. London: Barrie and Rockliff, 1951.

D. *Modern drama*

Brecht, Bertolt. "Galileo," *Seven Plays*. Edited by Eric Bentley. New York: Grove, 1961.

Brustein, Robert. *The Theatre of Revolt*. Boston: Little, Brown, 1964.

Büchner, Georg. "Danton's Death," *Complete Plays and Prose*. New York: Hill and Wang, 1963.

O'Neill, Eugene. *The Iceman Cometh*. New York: Vintage.

———. *A Long Day's Journey Into Night*. New Haven: Yale University Press, 1956.

E. *Relation of existentialism to radical theology*

Camus, Albert. *The Rebel*. New York: Vintage, 1958.

———. "The Unbeliever and Christians," *Resistance, Rebellion and Death.* New York: Knopf, 1961.

Earle, William. "Man Is the Impossibility of God" and "The Paradox and the Death of God," *Christianity and Existentialism.* Evanston: Northwestern University Press, 1963.

Edie, James M. "The Absence of God," *Christianity and Existentialism.* Evanston: Northwestern University Press, 1963.

Hopper, Stanley R. "On the Naming of the Gods in Holderlin and Rilke," *Christianity and the Existentialists.* Edited by Carl Michalson. New York: Scribner's, 1956.

Sartre, Jean-Paul. "Existentialism Is a Humanism," *Existentialism from Dostoevsky to Sartre.* Edited by Walter Kaufmann. Cleveland: Meridian, 1957.

———. *The Words.* New York: G. Braziller, 1964.

F. Psychoanalytical material related to the concerns of radical theology

Brown, Norman O. *Life Against Death.* Middletown: Wesleyan, 1959.

Freud, Sigmund. *Civilization and Its Discontents.* New York: Anchor, 1964.

———. *The Future of an Illusion.* New York: Anchor, 1965.

Fromm, Erich. *The Dogma of Christ.* New York: Holt, Rinehart & Winston, 1963.

Jung, C. G. *Aion: Researches into the Phenomenology of the Self* (Collected Works, vol. IX, part 2). New York: Pantheon, 1959.

———. *Answer to Job.* Cleveland: Meridian.

———. *Memories, Dreams, Reflections.* Edited by Ariela Jaffe. New York: Pantheon, 1963.

Marcuse, Herbert. *Eros and Civilization.* New York: Vintage, 1962.

Philip, H. L. *Jung and the Problem of Evil.* London: Barrie and Rockliff, 1958.

Rieff, Philip. *Freud: The Mind of a Moralist.* New York: Anchor, 1961.

G. "Radical" themes in modern Jewish theology

The first four titles represent a rather conservative approach to the concerns of radical theology, while the work of Rubenstein is perhaps the closest to it among Jewish scholars today.

Buber, Martin. *Eclipse of God.* New York: Torchbooks, 1957.

————. *I and Thou.* New York: Scribner's, 1958.

————. *Two Types of Faith.* New York: Torchbooks, 1961.

Fackenheim, Emil. "On the Eclipse of God," *Commentary*, June, 1964.

Rubenstein, Richard. "Person and Myth in the Judaeo-Christian Encounter," *Christian Scholar*, Winter, 1963.

————. "The Symbols of Judaism and Religious Existentialism," *The Reconstructionist*, May 1, 1959.

Taubes, Jacob. *See* articles on dialectical theology, *Journal of Religion*, January, April and October, 1954.

Taubes, Susan A. "The Absent God," *Journal of Religion*, Jan., 1955.

H. *Preparation for radical theology in Protestant neo-orthodoxy*

It is not easy to state correctly the relation between radical theology and liberalism on the one hand, and radical theology and neo-orthodoxy on the other. *Honest to God* was quite correct in pointing to the common influence of Bultmann, Tillich and Bonhoeffer.

1. Dietrich Bonhoeffer

Bonhoeffer, Dietrich. *Letters and Papers from Prison.* New York: Macmillan, 1962.

Secondary sources:

Bethge, Eberhard. "The Challenge of Dietrich Bonhoeffer's Life and Thought," *Chicago Theological Seminary Register*, February, 1961.

Dumas, André. "Dietrich Bonhoeffer et l'interpretation du Christianisme comme non-religion," *Archives de Sociologie des Religions*, Jan.-June, 1965.

Lochman, J. M. "From the Church to the World," *New Theology No. 1.* Edited by Martin Marty and D. G. Peerman. New York: Macmillan, 1964.

Mueller, Hanfried. "Concerning the Reception and Interpretation of Dietrich Bonhoeffer," *Die Muendige Welt*, IV.

————. *Von der Kirche Zur Welt.* Reich Evang. Verlag, 1961.

2. Rudolf Bultmann

Bultmann, Rudolf. "New Testament and Mythology," in *Kerygma and Myth.* New York: Torchbooks, 1961.

————. "The Idea of God and Modern Man," *Translating Theology into the Modern Age.* New York: Torchbooks, 1965.

Secondary sources:

Hobbs, Edward C., ed. *Stubborn Faith: Papers on Old Testament and Related Subjects*. Dallas: SMU Press, 1956.

Robinson, James M. and M. Noth, eds. *The Bultmann School of Biblical Interpretation: New Directions*. New York: Torchbooks, 1965.

3. Paul Tillich

Tillich, Paul. *The Courage to Be*. New Haven: Yale University Press, 1952.

————. *The Protestant Era*. Translated by James L. Adams. Chicago: University of Chicago Press, 1957.

————. *The Shaking of the Foundations*. New York: Scribner's, 1948.

————. *Systematic Theology*. 3 vols. Chicago: University of Chicago Press, 1963.

I. Radical theology in Europe

Lewis, John Wren. "Does Science Destroy Belief?" in *Faith, Fact and Fantasy*. London: Fontana, 1964.

Moltmann, J. *Theologie der Hoffnung*. Munich: Kaiser Verlag, 1965.

Robinson, John A. *Christian Morals Today*. Philadelphia: Westminster, 1964.

————. *Honest to God*. Philadelphia: Westminster, 1963.

————. *The New Reformation*. Philadelphia: Westminster, 1965.

Smith, Ronald Gregor. *The New Man*. London: SCM Press, 1956.

Solle, Dorothee. *Stellvertretung: ein kapital theologie nach dem "tode Gottes."* Kreuz-Verlag, 1965.

J. Studies on secularization

This is a vast field. Theological material on it is being published continually, and it is of interest to those other than theologians, radical or otherwise.

Cox, Harvey. *The Secular City*. New York: Macmillan, 1965. *See* Chapter 1.

Gogarten, F. *Der Mensch zwischen Gott und Welt*. Friedrich Vorwerk Verlag, 1956.

————. *Verhangniss und Hoffnung der Neuzeit*. Friedrich Vorwerk Verlag, 1953.

Hoekendijk, J. C. "On the Way to the World of Tomorrow," *Laity*, August, 1961.

"Secularization," *The Student World.* 1st Quarter, 1963.

Shiner, Larry. "Toward a Theology of the Secular," *Journal of Religion,* October, 1965.

Smith, Ronald Gregor. "A Theological Perspective of the Secular," *Christian Scholar,* March, 1960.

Van Leeuwen, A. *Christianity and World History.* London: Edinburgh House, 1964.

Von Weizsacker, C. F. *The Relevance of Science.* New York: Harper, 1965. *See* Chapter 10.

K. *Miscellaneous contemporary material pertaining to the idea of the death of God*

Bergman, Ingmar. *Silence, Through a Glass Darkly,* and *Winter Light.*

Fingarette, Herbert. *The Self in Transformation.* New York: Harper, 1964.

Goldmann, Lucien. *The Hidden God.* New York: Humanities, 1965.

Harrington, Michael. *The Accidental Century.* New York: Macmillan, 1965.

Kolakowski, Leszek. "The Priest and the Jester," *Dissent,* Summer, 1962.

L. *Descriptions, mostly from a sympathetic outsider's point of of view, of radical theology and its problems*

Cobb, John B. "From Crisis Theology to the Post-Modern World," *The Centennial Review,* Spring, 1964.

Funk, Robert W. "Colloquium on Hermeneutics," *Theology Today,* October, 1964.

Gilkey, Langdon B. "The God is Dead Theology and the Possibility of God-Language," *The Voice,* Crozier Theological Seminary, January, 1965. *Only portions available.*

―――. "Secularism's Impact on Contemporary Theology," *Christianity and Crisis,* April 5, 1965.

Reeves, Gene. "A Look at Contemporary American Theology," *Religion in Life,* Autumn, 1965.

Trotter, F. Thomas. "Variations on the Death of God Theme in Recent Theology," *Journal of Bible and Religion,* January, 1965.

M. *Books and articles representative of radical theology*

1. Herbert Braun

Braun, Herbert. "The Problem of New Testament Theology," *The*

Bultmann School of Biblical Interpretation: New Directions. Edited by James M. Robinson and others. New York: Torchbooks, 1965.

On Braun:

Gollwitzer, Helmut. *The Existence of God.* Philadelphia: Westminster Press, 1965. *See* pp. 35-51, 81-107.

2. David Miller

Miller, David. "False Prophets in the Secular City," *Christian Century,* November 17, 1965.

————. "Salvation and the Image of Comedy," *Religion in Life,* Summer, 1964.

————. "The Symbolizing of the Symbol," *Brethren Life and Thought,* Summer, 1963.

3. Gabriel Vahanian

Vahanian, Gabriel. "Beyond the Death of God," *Dialog,* Autumn, 1962.

————. *The Death of God.* New York: G. Braziller, 1961.

————. "The Future of Christianity in a Post-Christian Era," *The Centennial Review,* Spring, 1964.

————. "Swallowed Up by Godlessness," *Christian Century,* December 8, 1965.

————. *Wait Without Idols.* New York: G. Braziller, 1964.

4. Richard Underwood

Underwood, Richard, "Hermes and Hermeneutics: A Viewing from the Perspectives of the Death of God and Depth Psychology," *The Hartford Quarterly,* Fall, 1965.

5. Paul van Buren

Van Buren, Paul. "The Dissolution of the Absolute," *Religion in Life,* Summer, 1965.

————. "Linguistic Analysis and Christian Education," *Religious Education,* January-February, 1965. *Contains* a statement by van Buren and some responses. *See,* in particular, the response of Frederick Ferré.

————. *The Secular Meaning of the Gospel.* New York: Macmillan, 1963.

————. "Theology in the Context of Culture," *Christian Century,* April 7, 1965.